THE
INTREPID
BROTHERHOOD

GORDON GRAHAM
with **JOHN DESIMONE**

Public Power, Corruption, and
Whistleblowing *in the*
Pacific Northwest

THE
INTREPID
BROTHERHOOD

In Search Of Aristotle

info@in-search-of-aristotle.com
ISBN: 978-0-578-96143-9 (print)
ISBN: 978-0-578-99189-4 (ebook)

Cartoon Illustrations by Dan McConnell

Ordering Information:
Special discounts are available on quantity purchases by corporations, associations, and others. For details, contact:
In Search of Aristotle
info@in-search-of-aristotle.com
www.intrepidbrotherhood.com

Emotionally dedicated to my wife and best friend, Deanna;

In memory of my sister and my parents;

Specifically dedicated to Doug, Mark, Brian, and Scott Kane;

Affectionately dedicated to the "real" IT staff at Chelan County PUD;

Generally dedicated to every working soul who has labored under the conditions created by the all-too-common practice of constructive discharge.

DISCLAIMER

This book is a memoir. It reflects the author's recollections of experiences over time. No names have been changed, no characters invented, no events fabricated. The events related on the following pages are substantiated by no fewer than eight file boxes and countless electronic versions of records including (but not limited to): legal depositions, verbatim testimony, meeting records, investigative reports, clerk's notes, court rulings, email threads, newspaper archives, radio program transcripts and the personal recollections of some very sharp people. This memoir is a truthful recollection of actual events in the author's life. Some conversations may have been recreated and/or supplemented. The author of this book disclaims liability for any loss or damage suffered by any person as a result of the information or content in this book.

Why is it that the monsters among us so easily find willing disciples? It is because they are not the apparitions we expect them to be, but rather reflections of ourselves.

– Paraphrased from Peter Zrioka "The Monsters Among Us," Arizona State University Knowledge Enterprise, October 22, 2012

CONTENTS

Contents

INTRODUCTION

In Search of Aristotle

As of this writing, it has been more than ten years since the final judgment in my case. Some might think it healthier to put it behind me and forget about it—I have, and I haven't. The experiences I describe in this book are well in my rearview mirror, but as time passed, I got the nagging sense that I needed to tell my story. Forgiving and forgetting are two different psychological states. I didn't write this book to shame anyone, but to remember life lessons learned—ones I believe are worthy of passing on to another generation. My experiences, I believe, are also part of our community memory that is worth preserving.

This is the story of what can happen to a respectable organization and its people when the wrong leaders claim power. Most of the significant activities in this story occurred during a relatively narrow window of time during my 23 years at the Chelan County Public Utility District. Several events converged at a critical time. I had just completed my master's studies in Information Technology Management, and I was excited to apply many of the concepts I had learned to make my department more successful. Meanwhile, an individual steadily rose through the management ranks who eventually landed in the general manager's office. Our perspectives were so different in our management philosophies that we were destined to collide. How that collision took place and the toll exacted on my coworkers and myself is the subject of this book.

My perspective on managing people resulted from my exposure to modern writers on management practices. Many of them used materials and concepts established centuries ago by ancient philosophers and military leaders. Among those were Aristotle, from the fourth century BC, and Confucius from the fifth century BC. Both philosophers emphasized personal ethics in leadership. Authentic leaders exercise their moral authority above anything else. They don't depend on coercion or punishment to make employees feel committed to the corporate objectives. Instead, they motivate and reward them.

By contrast, toxic managers have an autocratic idea of power. That's why they aren't concerned about their behavior causing harm. They see the business or organization as a machine that needs to function correctly. Their subordinates are just cogs in the machine.

Well-known author Peter Drucker wrote that Aristotle referred to the solution to this conflict between the autocrat and the moral leader as the Ethics of Prudence—he says it is an "ethical duty for a leader to exemplify the precepts of ethics in his own behavior."[1] Drucker believed that leaders should adopt the personal philosophy of above all (or first) do no harm. He advised using "the mirror test" to ask yourself what person you want to see when you look into the mirror every morning. Based on these ancient principles, most modern writers on management topics believe there is only one set of ethics, one set of rules of morality or code of individual behavior, and the same rules apply to everyone. While I was trying to impart this concept of ethics in management to my leadership team in IT, a different philosophy was emerging in executive management. The new general manager had made his executive team aware that he was fond of a Chinese military strategist named Sun Tzu, who was alive at approximately the same time as Confucius. Sun Tzu wrote a series of notes compiled into a now-famous collection called *The Art of War*. Sun Tzu was primarily a military leader and wrote in military terms, but many of his strategies serve as a metaphor for modern business leadership practices. Indeed, his notes on military strategy are easily translated into competitive initiatives for business success.

I recently revisited an analysis of the leadership principles of Sun Tzu by Matt Harrison.[2] He acknowledges that there is no apparent correlation between Sun Tzu's notes and modern management principles. Harrison emphasizes that the instructions are a metaphor, and it is necessary to make the appropriate interpretation to apply their value to management

1 Peter Drucker, *The Changing World of the Executive* (New York: Truman Talley Books, 1982).
2 Matt Harrison, *Leadership Lessons from Sun Tzu and the Art of War*, read by Nate Sjol (Newark: Audible, April 2018), audiobook, 31 minutes.

principles. If a student of Sun Tzu does not translate his military principles into modern-day leadership concepts, and instead latches onto the military buzz words such as "discipline," "control," and "authority," they would come away believing that everything in business should be a battle. This, I believe, is what took place during the period I describe in this book.In my Information Technology department, we tried to promote practices taught by people like Peter Senge in his Learning Organization disciplines. Concepts such as shared visioning and team learning are used to cultivate individual ethics in management. At the same time, executive managers were running around talking about "winning decisive engagements quickly" and "defending existing positions." I believe this language, and the ensuing behavior it justified, resulted from their superficial perusal of Sun Tzu's teachings.

Such was the inevitable collision.

The sad part is that this conflict never had to happen. In reality, there is much that Sun Tzu and Aristotle had in common. Sun Tzu implored leaders to be an inspiration to subordinates and to lead by example. He cautioned leaders to treat subordinates with respect and kindness. His teachings instructed them to delegate tasks based on their subordinates' strengths and observed that "he who delegates a task to someone who has no strength in that discipline will surely fail." Likewise, he observed that groups are only as strong as their weakest link and that "without harmony in the state, consensus in the group, and well-being in the entire company," there can be no success. You will see how the failure to interpret these principles correctly is significant in this story.

In whatever manner Sun Tzu's teachings came to general management's attention, it is regrettable that they did not stumble on Aristotle's writings on ethics instead.

The most influential ideas of personal ethics extend back to the great philosopher and reach forward to guide effective managers today. This story is not only about what happened to me, but how my search for and use of management ethics guided me during some very challenging times.

Gordon Graham

February 2021

Chapter 1

Roll on Columbia
(or a Visionary Beginning)

The rugged geography of Washington State, its coulees, its eastern scablands, and the majestic Columbia River's winding course were carved out of the volcanic earth by repeated cycles of towering waves. For centuries, deluges from the Glacial Lake Missoula in Montana filled and emptied, pushing thundering floods of water and ice that scraped the land, shaping its massive drainage basin.[3] When the weather stabilized into what it is today, the ice melted, emptying into the fissures and coulees,

3 Montana Natural History Center, Glacial Lake Missoula Chapter of the Ice Age Floods Institute, "Glacial Lake Missoula and The Ice Age Floods," accessed July 23, 2021, https://www.glaciallakemissoula.org/.

creating the streams and rivers, and filling the meandering drainage beds that became the mighty Columbia River.

The Columbia River

Today, the Columbia River rises in the Canadian Rockies of British Columbia, turns northwest, then south. Its western terminus runs through a deep glacial gorge that forms the Oregon border, bounded by cliffs and forests, and empties its racing water into the sea. At over 1,200 miles long, it is the fourth longest river in America, and its drainage basin, with its streams and tributaries, is as large as France.[4] With its many drops and falls, its turbulent rapids and gorges, and its year-round volume, it was only natural that engineers searched for spots to build hydropower plants. They surveyed the banks of the Columbia, its reaches and gorges, for the most advantageous places to harness the river's forces.[5]

---

4 "Columbia River," Wikipedia, accessed June 14, 2021, https://en.wikipedia.org/wiki/Columbia_River.

5 John Harrison, "Dams: History and Purpose," Northwest Power and Conservation Council, https://www.nwcouncil.org/reports/columbia-river-history/DamsHistory; "Hydropower," https://www.nwcouncil.org/reports/columbia-river-history/Hydropower.

In 1889, two Washington State counties merged to create Chelan County with Wenatchee as its county seat. Chelan, a Native American word meaning "deep waters," is also a lake, one of the deepest in the nation, flowing in a 50-mile-long trench dug by glacial activity over 12,000 years ago.[6] The slip of water skirts the edges of the green Cascade Mountains, rimmed on both sides by fir trees that spill down to the edges of the sparkling water. Fed by the Stehekin River on its northern tip, water thunders down 400 feet into a precipitous ice-carved gorge before merging into the Columbia River at its southern terminus.

Just 40 miles downstream, at the confluence of the Columbia and Wenatchee Rivers, lies the burgeoning town of Wenatchee, a stop along the route of the Great Northern Railroad. The settlement of the district had been steady, and by 1904, about 4,000 residents lived in the area. With abundant water and a well-developed transportation system, but the land was arid and with little rainfall not suitable for farming unless it could be irrigated.

In 1904, Seattle investors built the Highline Canal, and the first 9,000 acres were put under cultivation, birthing the apple industry in Washington State. Influential voices, such as Rufus Woods, the Wenatchee Chamber of Commerce, and other business organizations, had their eyes on more significant projects. Surrounding the town to the west and south were over two million acres of arable land—it just needed water to irrigate it and electricity to power the pumps.

At the time, electricity to run irrigation pumps came from

---

6 Hu Blonk, *The Rock Island Dam Story* (Wenatchee: The Wenatchee World for Chelan County, 1975).

Puget Sound Power & Light. They had purchased the existing local operation from a predecessor and improved the lines and equipment, but at critical times, power was intermittent. It wasn't unusual during the irrigation season, with the pumps running all day and night, for the lights in homes and businesses to dim and go dark for hours. When the weather turned hot and water was critical, pumps often tripped off, with farmers losing a portion of the season's crops.

The demand for electricity outstripped supply and hindered the area's growth. And those demands could not be met alone from the western part of the state. Proposals to build hydroelectric dams along the Columbia to electrify homes and power irrigation pumps had been around for years. The Grand Coulee project upstream from Wenatchee had early been on developers' minds. But that location was controlled by the Washington Water Power and wouldn't benefit the Wenatchee area directly.[7]

The Great Northern Railroad controlled the Chelan gorge with its 400-foot drop, and it figured into their plans to construct the eight-mile-long Cascade Tunnel. They agreed with Washington Water Power to purchase the Chelan gorge to build a tunnel, dam, and power plant. The dam was completed in 1926, just in time to provide power for the electric locomotives of Great Northern's new line through the mountains.

Not one dam had been built yet on the Columbia River, but civic leaders foresightedly reserved Wenatchee's particular location. South of the city, 12 miles downstream, the Rock Island reach, bordered by basalt cliffs with two large boulders in the

7 Hu Blonk, *Behind The By=Line Hu: A Feisty Newsman's Memoirs* (Wenatchee: Self Published, 1992).

riverbed forming nearly unnavigable rapids, had been declared by engineers and local leaders a suitable site. With a high volume of water rushing through its rocky riverbed and prominent basalt outcroppings along the shorelines that indicated there would be solid footing for the dam's construction, engineers declared it the best location to build. Preliminary surveys of the site on several occasions had pronounced rich possibilities. A span across the rocky section could generate millions of dollars in revenue. A local dam would open up irrigation for the entire Quincy and Moses Lake areas. With abundant local supplies of electricity, lumber, and pulp mills, other industries would follow, bringing jobs and growth to the entire Wenatchee District.

For decades, rumors and fits of activity never moved a spade full of dirt on the project until 1928 when a manager for the Puget Sound Power & Light Company (PSP&L) visited the area. He announced that a permit had been filed with the state seeking the right to develop the site at Rock Island, and a federal permit would follow. The proposed project would raise the dam's water level, creating waterfront property for owners along the river. The PSP&L executive asked for help from the enthusiastic local trustees in gaining right-of-way for the dam and reservoir from the owners—all 275 landowners. The *Wenatchee World*, in a bold headline, announced the new project, inviting the landowners to come forward and agree to the PSP&L's terms. Enough landowners granted the right-of-way that the federal and state permits moved forward.

That March, Major John S. Butler, district engineer for the Corps of Engineers, came to town. He promoted the benefits of the dam in a series of meetings, stating that Rock Island was only the first of many projects on the federal government's drawing board. The Columbia possessed many development opportunities, and now was the time for the community to step forward. After his visit, excitement ran high among the citizens that the dam would finally be built.

As much as the business groups worked hard to sway the final decision, loud voices protested the permanent damage to the river's fish stocks. The numerous fishery agencies in Oregon and Washington, commissions, fish canneries, and just about every county fish and game conservationists cried out. Once the concrete barrier was erected across the river, the upstream salmon run would be cut off from their spawning grounds. Destroying the fish habitats would be permanent and detrimental.

PSP&L supervising engineers vehemently denied the dam's detrimental effects. With proper fish ladders and other accommodations, the fish wouldn't be harmed. Months of back-and-forth negotiation ensued between the supervising engineers and the protesters. Finally, on August 2, 1929, the Federal Power Commission issued a preliminary permit for the Rock Island project for a $20 million venture. The one provision was that the design would provide navigation and protection for the fish. In October, the FPC granted the actual license to construct the dam with the generated horsepower listed at 84,000.

Just as construction was about to begin, a new objection arose from a well-established group. The Washington State Grange, a powerful agricultural and political advocacy group, raised an entirely different issue in protesting the project. They were opposed to the private ownership and operation of electrical power in the state of Washington. They advocated for public ownership of all utilities, citing the abuses of the power trusts. Just the previous year, Congress had completed an exhaustive investigation of the "power trusts" operated by Sam Insull, a Chicago-based utility magnate. The federal investigation uncovered many improprieties and resulted in the collapse of his utility empire. Because of their extensive use of holding companies to stack utilities across the East Coast and the Midwest, they had very little capital investment in the operating companies. The collapse of Insull's power trust contributed significantly to the stock market crash later that year.

The Grange feared the rise of another "power trust" that would seek to control hydroelectric power across the entire nation, raising rates and returning usurious profits to the deep pockets of Wall Street investors.

Their alternative was to create public utility districts across the state, which would provide inexpensive and reliable power to farmers and rural households—something private utilities had done only sporadically.

The Grange's objections didn't stop the Rock Island Dam's construction, which commenced on schedule, and the first power was transmitted in November 1931.

Meanwhile, on the national front, Congress took legislative action and outlawed utility holding companies, forcing the divestiture of several of the companies in Washington. The holding companies fought back with drawn out court battles, and the final divestment of PSP& L and Washington Water Power wouldn't take place until after WWII.

Even though the Rock Island Dam had moved forward, the

Grange hadn't stopped its campaign for the public ownership of utilities. Sixteen years earlier, in 1912, the Grange had sponsored a series of reforms in the state, one of which was the public initiative system. Believing that a public utility initiative put to a public vote would be defeated because of the private utility companies' deep pockets, the Grange chose an alternative. An initiative backed by sufficient signatures could be presented directly to the legislature. On October 25, 1928, the Grange presented an initiative authorizing public utility districts' formation to the legislature. The state Senate voted it down the next February. Since the legislature offered no alternative, the measure was automatically placed on the statewide ballot for the 1930 general election. With time to organize, the Grange and other supporters sold the people on the advantages of publicly owned utilities. The initiative passed, and the Public Utility Districts Act became the law. While the passage of the act didn't break the power of private utilities, it did weaken their hold.

But it was another Grange-sponsored bill, the Bone Power Bill, sponsored by Senator Homer Bone of Tacoma, allowing municipally owned electric utilities to sell power beyond their city limits that solidified support for the PUD Act. The private-power industry forced a public vote on that law, and the voters approved it on November 6, 1934. Publicly owned generators could now compete for resources and customers across county boundaries, which set the stage for the battle of lawsuits.

Private-power operators challenged the PUD Act in court. It wasn't until 1936 that the Washington State Supreme Court handed down a final disposition in favor of the PUD Act. Significant skirmishes had been won, but the battle was far from over.

The Chelan County Public Utility District was officially formed in 1936. But it still didn't have any power generation, utility lines, substations, or distribution systems. Puget Sound Power & Light still controlled Rock Island Dam, and negotiations would go on for years before WWII intervened.

It wasn't until after WWII, in 1948, that Kirby Billingsley, a Chelan PUD Commissioner took with him U.S. Senator Warren Magnuson and Congressman Henry "Scoop" Jackson to the Oval Office to meet with President Harry Truman. Billingsley explained to the president the SEC and Federal Power Commission's orders to divest the Washington Water Power Company and Puget Sound Power & Light. The three men asked Truman to instruct the Secretary of the Interior, Julius A. Krug, to pressure the SEC to follow through with their demands for the holding companies to divest the two companies. Additionally, Billingsley was convincing that the PUDs needed the entire operating systems—transmission lines, power generating systems, and support facilities—to guarantee stable supplies to their customers. The pressure worked, but the private power industry fought back through the courts, further delaying Chelan PUD's aspirations.

The commissioners decided on a new strategy. Instead of purchasing the power system whole, they would work on parts they could acquire in the hopes that eventually, they would have an entire utility with generation plants, distribution, and transmission lines. After their latest court action failed, PSP&L agreed to sell its distribution system for Chelan County and part of Douglas County, but not the Rock Island Dam. Chelan acquired the electrical distribution lines for $8 million in 1948.

When Seattle informed PSP&L that it would not renew its franchise to provide power to the city, the power company decided it was time to sell its remaining assets. Chelan County PUD seemed like the logical buyer, but then Seattle's City Power Company offered them $25 million for the Rock Island Dam. This raised the hackles of the Chelan PUD supporters. If Seattle purchased the dam, none of the power produced by Rock Island, at its current capacity, would stay in Chelan County. Instead, its full production, which just matched the growing city's current daily needs, would be transferred to Seattle, leaving Wenatchee and its farmers without access to any reliable source of inexpensive power.

A somewhat convoluted battle for the dam followed. The cities of Tacoma and Kirkland asked for the right to purchase the dam, citing their needs. With so many competing demands, the Chelan commissioners, in a final maneuver to keep their power local, filed a condemnation suit canceling out all the competing claims and put the issue to rest.

Before the suit could be successfully litigated, the Korean War intervened, and the nation's industrial base moved to a war footing. The government needed more electrical generation to expand the nation's aluminum industry, and Washington State was a primary location to find that power. The government had tapped the Rock Island area as a suitable location to build a much-needed aluminum plant. But Rock Island, in its present configuration, with only one of its powerhouses built out, didn't have the capacity to power both Seattle and the new Alcoa plant.

PSP&L would need to build out the rest of the dam to meet all the projected demand. But because its license to service

Seattle was set to expire, it couldn't tap the bond market to raise the capital necessary to finance the construction. The federal government came in strong, threatening to take over the dam and its output if the various entities didn't agree to solve their ownership issue.

Thanks to the farsighted PUD commissioners, such as Kirby Billingsley, they stepped in and negotiated a creative four-way solution to the problem. A public-private-federal partnership would serve as a template for other PUDs to follow in building out their generation systems. Chelan PUD would lease the dam's unused sections and then borrow the funds to build out the remaining powerhouses, expanding the output from 80,000 to 255,000 kilowatts. The power would be sent to Puget Sound to service its obligations. Then the federal government came to the table with an agreement to use Bonneville Dam's capacity to meet Alcoa's needs to operate their aluminum plant. Chelan County would be the site of a large Alcoa plant and begin operating its first dam. Eventually, it would purchase Puget Sound's portion of the dam and build out the third section in 1979, making Rock Island Dam operational.

Rock Island Dam

The private-public-federal partnership arrangement pioneered by Chelan PUD Commissioners served as the Eisenhower Administration's model to build dams across the country. Chelan PUD would use it later in the decade to develop its third and final dam project at Rocky Reach upstream.

Rocky Reach Dam

Before that happened, the Chelan PUD made another acquisition. In 1955, with $26 million from a bond issue, it purchased Lake Chelan Hydro from Washington Water Power (now Avista Corp).

Lake Chelan Dam

Chelan PUD commissioned Rocky Reach Dam, a site on the Columbia about seven miles upstream from Wenatchee, to complete its system. These were the Eisenhower years of industrial and agricultural expansion. Permits were issued and construction began in 1956. The first phase was completed in 1959.

It took 23 years for Chelan County to realize its dream of harnessing local resources to create a public utility that could produce reliable and inexpensive power, a utility accountable to the people through an elected board of local citizens. The multi-decade struggle to produce enough electric power within the county to meet the growing population's needs and expand the community's industrial base, bringing jobs and tax revenues into the community, was handsomely rewarded with an operational PUD. The aggregate generating kilowatt power of the three facilities made it the largest PUD in the state and the second-largest non-federal publicly owned hydroelectric generating system in the nation.

The hallmark of this achievement is that it was accomplished by farsighted men and women who had the best interests of the community at heart. Since its formal organization in 1948, Chelan County PUD has been led by a series of homegrown managers, mostly from the Wenatchee area. All the general managers in the first 60 years of operation—seven in total— had either been engineers or accountants who had worked their way up through the organization. The men who rose through the ranks to fill the general manager's position had earned the respect and support of their peers and colleagues. In most cases, they were community leaders with extensive involvement in local electric power issues.

I didn't now know any of them personally, but from what I've learned of them, they were all known as people who lived by one set of values. In Aristotle's terms, they were "moral leaders" who led by example and not by coercion. These men were not only visionaries who built an organization to serve the future needs of a growing community. They were leaders who knew how to motivate workers and reward achievement. They fostered a collegial atmosphere of open communications, much like what one would experience in a functional family. The corporate atmosphere was that it was "like a family." A functional family trusts each other, lives by one set of shared values, and recognizes and encourages each individual's talent.

The commissioners were cut from the same cloth. They were local people, small-town pragmatists—orchardists, educators, and businesspeople. Most of the employees knew each other, had attended school with each other, and often attended church together, giving the company a sense of connection with the community. The entire structure of energy production and distribution was purposely built to serve the people and facilitate the local economy's development.

≋⌇≋

When I returned to Wenatchee in 1981 to interview for a position with the Chelan County PUD, I had been away from the area for 12 years. I had moved to Western Washington to attend college, and after graduating I worked at various data processing and programming jobs on the coast. When my wife and I had decided to move closer to our roots, Wenatchee stood out as a wonderfully safe and healthy place to raise our growing family.

Taking a position at the Chelan County PUD fulfilled a dream to work for a company that closely held the community's values. It wasn't difficult to discern that the Chelan County PUD was a local operation that embodied specific values: collaboration, communication, mutual support, and honesty, among others. Accepting a position at the PUD in 1981, I felt confident I could grow my career and my family.

Over the next two decades, I enjoyed progressively more responsible assignments and positions within the department. My experience and jobs touched on almost every aspect of business processes, and I enjoyed mastering new technologies and applications that were steadily improving data processing. Eventually, our department name even took on a new luster, keeping with the trend to reflect the department's transformation, changing its name from Information Systems to Information Technology, shortened to the now-familiar IT department.

In 1997, Sonny Smart, the GM for the past four years, announced his retirement. In his 37-years with the firm, he had begun his career as an engineering aide assigned to the Rocky Reach Dam and moved through the ranks until taking the GM spot four years before. By 1997, Parkinson's had begun to sap his vigor, and he filed his retirement papers that October. In some of his last remarks before he stepped down, he stated that times had changed, and he called for a new type of GM who could address the national issues facing the PUD, such as the deregulation of the energy market.[8] His insight would prove prescient about the leadership the organization needed—someone who knew more than how to deal with bond issues, the employee count, and fishery issues. Upon his retirement, the commissioners unanimously agreed to post a nationwide search for a new GM, someone who could lead the growing public energy company into the future.

8 "2000-01 California Electricity Crisis," Wikipedia, accessed June 14, 2021, https://en.wikipedia.org/wiki/2000-01_California_electricity_crisis.

Chapter 2

Then Whence Cometh Evil?

Why the national search didn't move forward is shrouded in a bit of PUD mystery. We can only surmise they were talked out of commissioning such a search. What we do know is the name of the primary instigator behind that decision. His name was Charlie Hosken, who, at the time, was the PUD's treasurer.

I initially only knew him in passing and by reputation. Charlie was known within the organization to have high aspirations of one day becoming the general manager. He had voiced this on more than one occasion to coworkers. While it is admirable from a career perspective when a person has lofty goals and views promotions as just rewards for top performance, people who knew Charlie perceived that he considered his rise up the corporate ladder differently—more as a grab for power. Grasping and holding power would prove to be his central preoccupation, a bent of character that would come to dominate his tenure in top management and sow seeds of havoc throughout the organization.

Hired in 1992 as an auditor straight from Deloitte & Touche, Hosken, had a frumpy frame with thinning hair, a blonde mustache, and a pugnacious way about him that put fellow workers on edge and kept them there. His round face was dominated by a long slanting nose, which he used as a tool to glare down disdainfully at anyone who crossed him. At times, he could be arrogant, overly confident, secretively calculating, and with such high regard for his own opinions, it would have torn out his very soul if he ever thought he could be wrong. As my experience with him will prove in this story, those he couldn't control didn't work around him for long. One of the best ways to frame his insatiable ambition is to think of Shakespeare's Macbeth, a man who created chaos to slake his thirst for control and left a prodigious body count in his wake.

In his first position, Hosken worked as an internal auditor under John Beatty, the treasurer. Beatty came to the PUD in 1985 with a solid record of handling bond issues. Because of his relationships with the New York bond market, Beatty had standing instructing by the commissioners to borrow as much cash as he could during periods of low interest rates. By stretching the bond terms years into the future, the PUD had accumulated a sizable reserve of cash they would need to finance infrastructure projects. They considered the increasing debt load as one the organization could handle because of the steady rise in demand for power in the district and the forecasted increases in new energy contracts staff were negotiating for the PUD's excess power.

The commissioners believed the reserves were essential to accomplishing the long-range goals of capital improvement and development required to meet the region's growing demand for power.

Sometime during 1993, Hosken presented to the commissioners the results of his audit. The PUD faced a drop in revenues and needed to increase rates across the board. Hosken pointed to the increasing debt burden and interest payments that now totaled $31 million per year as a significant reason for the unbalanced budget. Hosken maintained that the PUD had borrowed too much money. With only 18 percent of debt payments going to principal, leaving a whopping 82 percent of all payments going to interest, the PUD, in the eyes of the New York bonding agencies, possessed a "weak debt structure."

Hosken had been in contact with the bonding agencies back east who had sounded an alarm. He warned the commissioners that the organization's bond rating was in jeopardy of being downgraded if the interest to principal payments wasn't brought back into balance.

Hosken may have magnified the urgency of the issue, expertly playing a weak hand in his own Game of Thrones into a position of power. He was insistent before the commissioners that the PUD needed to slow down its borrowing and pay down its debt. There is no public record of the insinuations he made about his boss, John Beatty, but they must have been severe enough—most likely impugning the man's judgment and ability to perform his job. His warning so effectively destroyed the commissioners' trust in the very competent John Beatty that they decided upon drastic action.

Without accusing Beatty of mishandling or misappropriating funds, the commissioners voted to put the treasurer on paid leave and launch an investigation. They locked his office door and went into a private executive session to determine his fate.

The general manager at the time, Sonny Smart, wasn't involved in the deliberations, as the treasurer like the GM reported directly to the commissioners and not to the general manager.

The debate lasted a few weeks. Some of it was in public, but most of the critical decision-making was done in private. A few of the commissioners were troubled by the news from New York, but others were certain this was the ordinary course of business and were clear they had instructed Beatty to take on the debt at an advantageous interest rate.

However, after private consultations with the district's legal counsel and Beatty's lawyers, the full commission decided to part ways with John Beatty. They offered him a substantial severance of $92,000. That year, Charlie Hosken was promoted to Beatty's position as the new treasurer, in charge of dealing with new bond issues and PUD finances.

The shroud of secrecy surrounding the deliberations over Beatty's termination and severance was partially pierced by the *Wenatchee World*, reporting the severance payment had been approved during private discussions—a move that didn't sit well with the community. The response from the commissioners, and Sonny Smart, was that if the proceedings had been made public, their bond rating would have suffered. Wherever the truth lay, the secret deliberations vaulted Charlie Hosken into a top executive slot reporting directly to the commissioners. Just the control he so much craved.

I had no interaction with Hosken during his time as treasurer except for one decision that affected my job directly. He recommended and hired a friend he had worked with at Deloitte, Greg Larsen, and appointed him Management Information Systems (MIS/IT) Director.

≋⃒≋

Charlie Hosken had been the CFO for three years when Sonny Smart resigned in 1997. Hosken may have sensed the time wasn't right for him to make a big move for the top spot, as he didn't have enough of the commissioners on his side. So, he sought an intermediate step. He talked the outside counsel, Roger Braden, an accomplished and well-respected regulatory attorney in Wenatchee, who had worked closely with Chelan PUD on many issues, into applying for the position.

As the CFO and reporting directly to the five-person commission, Hosken had enough weight with the decision-makers to convince them that they should seriously consider a local candidate. Roger Braden had represented the utility in legal matters and relicensing issues for much of the past decade and had vast experience in the electric utility business in the Northwest. Braden was well-respected within the PUD, and Hosken likely made the case that bringing someone in from the outside could be risky when they had such a highly qualified candidate nearby. It would only come to light later that Hosken had solicited Roger Braden to apply for the GM position with the idea he would serve for five years and then step aside in favor of Hosken.

The commission called off their national search, hired Braden in July 1997. In February 1998, Braden appointed Hosken Executive Director of Generation, responsible for all excess power sales. It was in that department his reputation for fickleness and intemperate behavior began to spread.

He worked closely with Bill Dearing, a longtime PUD employee in charge of power marketing. There were many incidents during negotiations with outside power purchasers and other utilities. After the contracts he had approved were signed, Hosken often asked to revisit the terms, sometimes claiming he never agreed to the terms he had signed off on. Bill sensed the man feared his own decisions. If he had made a mistake or misjudged the market, he never wanted to be at fault. The contract staff called it managing by chaos. If there weren't problems, Hosken would stir one up, keeping everyone on edge and uncertain about what he'd do next.

This pattern of management style would repeat itself throughout his tenure.

In September of 1998, Braden promoted Hosken to Chief Operating Officer (COO). Braden stayed to his specialty of relicensing and contract negotiations, which he would have overseen anyway as the outside legal counsel, while Hosken effectively ran the day-to-day operations.

Hosken planned to move Braden aside when the right moment arose. The move would be mutual, and as a reward for his short tenure, Hosken had negotiated a lucrative severance agreement for the lawyer. That agreement would come into play later when Hosken believed he had enough votes on the board of commissioners to win an appointment to the top spot.

As the COO with all the departments under his control, Hosken's tenure in this position and later, as GM, ushered in a new management style. Not the collaborative win-win style of the community leader but a new, control-centric style that practically terrorized those who stood in his way.

≋⌷≋

Hosken appointed Greg Larsen as the new Chief Financial Officer (CFO), which he was much more suited for than managing Information Technology. With Larsen's elevation, his old position as Director of IT opened up. That's where I come in. I had been with Chelan County PUD now 16 years, working in several IT department capacities with increasing responsibility. With my education, experience, and job performance, I applied for the open position and was appointed the new department director. As the IT director, I became more actively involved in the industry, attending conferences and industry workshops. With the constant change and innovation in technology, I prided myself on incorporating the industry's best practices and creating an efficient, modern, and responsive department.

My promotion to department director came amid our preparations for the Y2K rollover to a new century. The concern throughout the IT industry indirectly and to our organization directly was palpable. Our technology had to pass muster for the benefit of our utility customers and our internal customers. From electrical generation to customer billing to accounts payable, every department depended on IT's a seamless transition to a new century. I traveled to London to meet with our insurance underwriters, Lloyd's of London and Zurich Insurance, attended industry trade associations, utility peer associations, local ratepayers forums, and service industry meetings. We needed to stay on the cutting edge of innovation and take every step to be well prepared for any eventuality. We'd never faced a transition with such a high degree of uncertainty. As a team, IT did everything we could to allay the fears and be ready for any eventuality.

As the new director with over 20 years of IT experience under my belt, I was increasingly aware of the trends in the organization's dependence on technology. Demands for the department's services were expanding along with the types and quantities of information we were asked to supply. The electrical energy generation industry was in the very beginning stages of deregulation, and we as an organization were reevaluating our role. Because the PUD had an uncertain regulatory future, it was leaning on new technology. So, requests for services and data were flooding our department, putting us always behind the curve of their needs, ever on the defensive trying to solve problems that hadn't existed before.

My analysis of the process was that it was dysfunctional. The IT department could no longer be considered an afterthought, just a bunch of computer nerds in the basement fooling around with their machines. Instead, if IT and its resources were fully integrated into the entire PUD's overall strategic planning, we could develop comprehensive solutions faster and more effectively. In my opinion, the IT department needed to have a seat at the executive table as full partners in the organization. I had researched this topic extensively and written papers on it for our industry meetings, so I was confident that my views were in keeping with what other utilities were doing. With Y2K looming and a new leader at the helm, now was the time to discuss my ideas with Charlie Hosken.

Prior to approaching Charlie Hosken with my concerns about the direction of the utility, I was still trying to work on my proposals for improvement in our strategic planning process through the existing management hierarchy. My boss at the time was Dick Nason, a man who had a somewhat puzzling progression to the executive level from previous assignments in the Fish and Wildlife Department. He was put in charge of Shared Services. These departments provide services commonly shared by every other department in the organization: Information Technology, Fleet Services, Risk Management and Accounting, and other similar functions. It is generally acknowledged that these departments don't contribute directly to the bottom line but are considered overhead to a degree.

No pun intended but, considering his background, Dick was a fish out of water. He wanted desperately to succeed at that level but didn't appear to be willing to invest the time and effort to learn how. For example, he indicated to all his subordinate directors that we would implement service level agreements with the departments we served. He requested that all of us submit templates for review and that we would choose the best one and move forward establishing service level commitments to each of our "customers." No orientation, no education, no recognition of the requirements for successful service level contracts. Just find a form and make your resources fit it. Since service levels were an integral part of the methodologies we were studying and promoting within my department, I asked to meet with

Dick several times to discuss the potential downside of hastily adopting a support strategy without proper preparation and knowledge. He was so anxious to convey to the manager and his executive peers that he had checked this off his "to do" list that he refused to listen.

Besides, he said, there was a new management philosophy emerging at his level. He said that Charlie, who was Chief Operating Officer at the time, was promoting strategies from *The Art of War* by Sun Tzu. He made it clear that his impression of this philosophy was "give no quarter and take no prisoners."

I was familiar enough with Sun Tzu's legacy to know that was not the primary message the ancient Chinese general was trying to convey. However, this perspective began to permeate the entire executive layer. It became clear to me that we would not reap any positive benefits.

During the fall of 1998, I asked for and received a meeting with the new COO. A tradition within our organization allowed employees to ask for a private after-hours discussion with an executive to address issues and concerns in an off-the-record conversation, a long-standing practice called "beer immunity." I had never used it before, but I believed the time had come to elevate my concerns about the department I'd worked in for nearly two decades.

During my first and only sit-down with Hosken at a local restaurant, I gave him some reasons why I believed IT's role within the organization needed to expand and become more fully integrated into the utility's strategic planning. I spoke to him about the benefits we had realized within my department by establishing collaborative management principles like shared visioning and team learning. I suggested that the entire company could benefit from adopting similar techniques and that the failure to do so could be catastrophic. I pointed out how difficult it was for a support organization to respond to expectations when they were so elusive and amorphous. I suggested a new position of Chief Information Officer (CIO) who could take a seat at the executive level, but I made it clear it didn't have to be me. I could see the wheels turning behind his eyes. He didn't say anything until I mentioned that the way we're currently operating made us look dysfunctional—always behind the curve instead of leading the way.

His reaction reminded me of a cat rearing back in anticipation of a fight, hair bristling along his spine. He took affront to my insinuation that any organization under his leadership could be dysfunctional. There was a sense he took my comments personally, as opposed to the way I presented them, as an opportunity to improve the performance of our entire organization.

Had I overstepped the boundaries of some unspoken protocols—not to bring up difficult subjects? I had always been told "beer immunity" meant just that. Nothing would be held against me. But from his evident reaction, I feared everything had changed. I went from someone he hardly knew and cared about—the man in the basement who ran all the computers— to someone to fear, and possibly much, much more.

I thought there might be repercussions, but never in my imagination did I expect what unfolded.

A short time after our meeting, Hosken went right to work stamping his way of conducting business on the entire enterprise. As an experienced auditor, he resorted to his best and most potent tool, an outside expert's objective opinion. Looking back, I realized it was the same way he stripped John Beatty of his position and power, blaming the New York bonding agencies who threatened to downgrade the PUD's credit rating because of the treasurer's imprudent borrowing.

Hosken commissioned performance improvement reviews of all corporate services departments, selecting Navigant Consulting for the job. The apparent motivation, the message that came down to the departments, was that the new executives were looking for services they could outsource. A way of cutting back on the budget, already strained to the point rate increases, was imminent. But employees got the sense Hosken wanted to get dirt on managers he didn't like—dirt he could use to demote or fire them. Producing chaos and uncertainty was something he did with such great skill and enthusiasm—it became a hallmark of his management style.

Whether the commissioners would allow departments such as IT to be outsourced wasn't something I considered when Navigant, a reputable management consulting company, showed up to audit my department. Working closely with the consultant, I was determined that the audit would be as thorough and objective as possible. The consultant had my assurances that everyone in our department would cooperate and participate in providing data for the report.

With the audit process completed, Navigant compiled its assessment and presented its findings to our department before submitting them to the executive board. The results were what

I had anticipated. The Navigant representative's full report was very positive in all the key areas, including its recommendation that outsourcing our department would cost more and not less. A conclusion many of us already knew. We were a lean operation, providing services that matched or exceeded the industry's best practices, with a robust feedback system with all the organizations' stakeholders. There was a certain amount of hope the report, which glowed with subdued praise for the entire IT operation, would put to rest any ill will Hosken harbored against the department in general and me in particular.

The presentation to the executive committee was set for November 17, 1999. I accompanied the Navigant staff to present the customer service survey results and answer any questions. The presentation went well—the upbeat report that the PUD had a highly efficient and capable IT department prepared to meet the entire operation's technology needs should have elicited smiles and praise. After the presentation, the presenter and I were stunned at the blank stares and total silence. There was not one question or comment. Just frowns.

My stomach dropped, and I held my breath, not wanting to show my shock at their reaction.

It was as if they had anticipated a bad report and, upon hearing good news, were too choked up even to speak. Had someone poisoned their opinion of what to expect? Did receiving a glowing report not fit with their plans, or was this something personal between Hosken and me?

Both of us left the meeting, walking in silence along the corridor. Finally, the consultant turned to me and asked, "What just happened in there?"

I could only shrug. I told him that it looked like their preconceived notions would not allow them to accept good news. Things were not going to get better, that much I knew. What I didn't realize was how low Hosken could go.

Not too long after I met with Hosken for beer, my wife and I were in the Wenatchee airport waiting for a plane to travel somewhere on business. I noticed a young man who worked in our accounting department across the room, and realized I had never spoken to him. I rose and approached him to introduce myself. With barely veiled disdain, he responded that he knew who I was. I inquired if he was traveling for business, and he avoided the question. I told him where I was headed and tried to make small talk, but he was visibly uncomfortable. He finally stood up and faced me directly. He said that he was going to a Chief Information Officer (CIO) training course. He had approached Charlie Hosken with the observation that our organization needed a CIO to oversee the strategy and direction of information technology.

I smiled, and I don't think he was expecting that.

I asked him if Charlie had told him that was my idea, since I had been recommending integrating technology at the strategic planning level for years. He said, "No, he didn't." By this time, the young man got agitated, clenched his fists, and rocked back and forth on his heels. I said that I had been pushing that idea for a long time and that I was thrilled that it was finally getting some consideration at the executive level. I wished him luck and offered to compare notes and push his agenda forward when he returned. He exhaled deeply and, without uttering a word, turned and walked away.

My wife, Deanna, witnessed the entire exchange, and afterward, said, "That young man thought he was going to have to hit you. He thought there was going to be a physical confrontation."

That this young man would take such a defensive standing toward me proved that Charlie didn't have anything positive to say about me. *The Art of War* had begun to seep into the workplace to the point he felt a need to clench his fists in readiness to hit me. That was the new environment Charlie Hosken brought to the PUD.

≋◫≋

Hosken continued to clean house. He pushed his friend, Greg Larsen, out of his CFO position over a dispute about rates. The PUD's revenues continued to be strained, and Larsen took the position with the commissioners that it was time for another rate increase, something Hosken didn't want.

He continued to move people around like so many chess pieces on the board, taking employees who had plateaued or eliminated positions and created new slots for them. In my estimation, staff who had plateaued in one job or whose jobs had been eliminated shouldn't have been top candidates for new and vital functions. If they hadn't kept their skills and knowledge current and weren't growing in one position, what made Hosken think they would excel in another slot? The only reason I could surmise he kept them around was that he had a hold on them. They either did his bidding or they would be out the door, just like his friend Greg Larsen. This would become apparent as Hosken's next phase of reshaping the PUD to his will got underway.

In 2001, the entire executive team gathered for a corporate retreat in Port Ludlow, a resort community on the West Coast. Because of the discussions' sensitive nature, Hosken and Braden decided that the meeting minutes would not be made public, as was usually the case.

In the ensuing weeks after the retreat ended, concerns were leaked to the local press, The *Wenatchee World*, that part of the reason for the secrecy was discussions had included the rationale for privatizing the PUD. After unsuccessful attempts to obtain the minutes directly, the *World's* editors jumped on that rumor and filed a freedom of information request. After that was denied, they sued under the Freedom of Information Act (FOIA) statute, and sadly, they lost. The judge determined the statute didn't cover the type of information they had requested.

While this was going on, someone at the PUD posted the retreat's minutes—whether it was inadvertently or purposefully was never determined—on the company's website. It was only up for a few hours before top brass demanded its removal, but it was just long enough for an astute reporter at the *Wenatchee World* to download it.

The cat was out of the bag, and in subsequent articles the truth came out. As the minutes of the meeting showed, the purpose of the retreat was twofold. It began with a discussion on how best to restructure the PUD to meet the emerging market forces unleashed through deregulation. Concerns were voiced that deregulation could result in a hostile takeover of the PUD. To prevent such an event, the organization needed to operate more like a commercial generator and not a citizen-owned public utility. Whether that meant they planned on finding a way to privatize the operation and strip it of its citizen ownership wasn't clarified. But the fact that privatization of a prized local utility came up in a discussion of the top-level leaders, when it became public in the ensuing months, would cause a firestorm of controversy.

The final item on the Ludlow retreat agenda was the announcement that the organization would be undergoing a reorganization centered on a new technology initiative called Enterprise Resource Planning (ERP). According to the meeting minutes, Hosken and Braden had been working on this reorganization for a while. Three individuals, ones removed from former positions, had been assigned full-time to the project, with another three in the works. In the words of Hosken and Braden, the ERP assignment was a "career determining" project. If they failed at implementing the ERP across the entire enterprise, their careers would be in the toilet, possibly not only with Chelan County PUD.

As Hosken and Braden saw it, the problem was that there were too many stand-alone information systems throughout the organization. According to them, systems were cobbled together that lacked integration. The current way of compiling and accessing information represented the "old ways of doing things." It was labor-intensive and didn't provide the data departments needed to make timely decisions. Hosken wanted instant and consistent access to common information so managers could act aggressively in the continually evolving energy business.

The deep irony of Hosken's plan was that this was precisely what I had spoken to him about almost two years before at the "beer immunity" session. When he had bristled at my suggestions that IT needed to become fully integrated into the PUD's strategic planning, I thought it would never happen. And now, instead of consulting with me or anyone in my department, he had appointed three termed out employees whose skills and knowledge no longer served their former job description. None of them had any experience or formal training in IT. Yet, they were charged with heading up a massive and expensive technology project with company-wide implications. Hosken wanted the old ways of doing things to be phased out and new ways of thinking brought in. Staff in charge of the project were told this was a career-defining project. Their success would be measured by how effective they were in pushing the old ways out the door.

It wasn't difficult for me to understand that "old ways" was a euphemism for "old employees," specifically IT employees.

The other point to keep in mind here is the warning by Sun Tzu to "delegate tasks based on their subordinates' strengths" and that "he who delegates a task to someone who has no strength in that discipline will surely fail." So, Charlie Hosken was planning to implement my vision for enterprise-level IT integration without my involvement. He then intended to put people in charge of that initiative with no practical strengths or experience in that discipline.

While the ERP program didn't raise any public hackles, the talk of privatizing the PUD, removing the citizen-owned component, stirred up a storm of protest until it became apparent there had to be a public sacrifice to appease the critics. Roger Braden, who had pretty much "retired in place" as some of those working directly with him had quipped, decided to take the fall. He resigned but didn't leave empty-handed. Because all large transactions become public information, Braden's lucrative $540,000 golden parachute, which he had negotiated in secret with Hosken before taking the position, was paid out, further incensing public opinion over the PUD leadership.

$25,000 PAY RAISE FOR PUD CEO ROGER BRADEN

With Braden out of the way, the organization needed a new

leader. The word in the company gristmill was that Hosken thought he had enough votes on the commission to get the job. But wanting to show fairness, commissioners decided they couldn't just crown Hosken the new emperor. His coronation needed to have at least some plausibility of objectivity.

Wayne Wright, a long-term PUD employee, stepped forward and threw his hat in the ring as a viable candidate. Wright was well-regarded within the organization, someone who had worked his way up the ladder, a meticulous communicator with a much warmer personality, an overall good fit for the old culture of congenial cooperation. The culture that Hosken was doing his best to sweep away.

The commissioners sanctioned a series of candidate forums, both for employees and the public. Both candidates were available to answer questions, discuss issues, and talk about their future vision. Resorting to this method of choosing the next general manager was unprecedented. It smacked of a gratuitous effort to make their vote appear to be the result of a popular referendum. But that wasn't typically how they made decisions.

After the public beauty contest wrapped up, the commission went into session and elected Hosken the next general manager, on a three to two vote. December 17, 2001, marked a dark day for the PUD that only those under the heel of his boot truly understood.

Later that day, Hosken showed up at an ERP meeting in the large conference room. Ron Clanton and Victor Reyez of AMS Consultants, his friends and former colleagues, accompanied him. Hosken was beaming when he announced his appointment as the new general manager. Steve Currit, a man I had little dealings with at the time, spoke up: "Let me be the first to kiss your ring."

According to someone in the room, Hosken responded: "That's not my ring you're kissing."

With this tone in mind, the Hosken era began.

Those who were willing to kiss the ring prospered. Those who did not need to kiss the ring, because they were under the illusion that their superior job performance would make room for them, were harassed until they quit or were fired. But that is the rest of the story.

In September of 2001, I was awarded an MBA in Information Technology Management from City University in Bellevue, Washington. Obtaining an advanced degree in my field of specialty was essential to me. Graduate level managers in information technology are "management generalists." They manage manpower, machines, and money the same as any other manager. The difference is that they are also tasked with managing technology. So, I understood the dynamics of what would make our organization successful as much as any other manager in any other department. With the fast pace of change and innovation in the industry, maintaining a sophisticated understanding of things like customer service programs and processes, and project management components were essential to the career I enjoyed and had dedicated myself to.

Like any department, we had a budget, and it was my job to see that we completed projects and tasks within our financial constraints. Bringing all our projects to closure and meeting our customers' needs for services without overspending was something I was very proud of and kept a close watch on.

During my leadership, I'd initiated the first Information Technology strategy in the history of the organization. The effort analyzed governance, economy, architecture, organization structure, and services to produce a comprehensive strategy. At my initiation, we developed a Business Information Technology Alignment Committee to represent the governance body for IT investments. As crucial as those accomplishments were, I also led my entire department's transition from an internally focused technical support department to a client-focused strategic partner. Gaining support and recognition for this issue was a significant accomplishment because IT is often seen as just one of many support services. But achieving the transition was monumental.

I was also active in the industry, contributing to industry conferences. Besides serving on numerous local boards, I served as the co-chair of the Information Technology Committee for the Northwest Public Power Association, as well as chair of the Information Technology Committee, and subsequently as the vice-chair of the Business and Finance Committee for the American Public Power Association. I was busy and enjoyed it immensely because I was engaged in things I loved doing and understood very well.

I expected changes after Hosken officially took over as the general manager, but I didn't know how and when they would take place. Not until my new supervisor, Wayne Wright, appeared at my door. With a look of concern on his face, he said we needed to have a conversation.

As the losing party in the general manager competition, Wayne Wright had been assigned to manage my department. Hosken had briefed him on what he perceived as the shortcomings of the IT department, and he came with an apparent agenda. I knew that Wayne was his own man—facts meant something to him. I fished the Navigant report out of my files and asked him to let me show him the facts. Navigant was the outside consultant hired by Hosken and his team to assess my department. I went through the 37-page report page by page and gave him a detailed explanation of our operation, efficiency, budget utilization, and other vital facts. The department had been rated above average out of all utilities our size and larger through an objective analysis. I toured him through the department, showing him the customer service reports, the state-of-art software we use to track service calls, the documentation we kept on each completed work order request. The comprehensive tour touched on every aspect of the department—our training programs, our project management tracking, our new technology initiatives, and our strategic plans for the next iteration of services. I could tell he was impressed.

It was a subdued and somewhat apologetic Wayne who left my department. I was hopeful once again that reality had refuted perception and that we were on our way to redemption and emerging from the cloud of controversy that had been created around us.

Instead, my colleagues and I would soon face a new threat—one we had no frame of reference for understanding until it was too late.

CHAPTER 3

Let Them Eat Cake

When Wayne Wright entered my office for the second time, he again had been sent by Charlie Hosken to deliver a message. Hosken had decided on a new structure that would place the department under a new supervisor—a new position called an Enterprise Technology Solutions (ETS) manager. And he made it clear that I would not be filling that position. My task was to nominate a person to take the job. The IT staff and I were to select this new manager whom we would report to. I took the news in stride. I didn't believe Hosken had suddenly developed a warm feeling for me after Wayne's first visit, but I did have a new flicker of hope that he had finally realized how vital and well run our department was. The fact I didn't at the time suspect any ulterior motives in this new tactic spoke to my misunderstanding of the entire predicament I was in. It just didn't seem plausible to me that one man would spend so much energy on being diabolical. I had a lot to learn. By including us in the decision-making process, the move seemed like a non-threatening way to announce a new structure, and to make it look like it was our idea. At least if the new director turned out to be less than we expected they would be able to say, "Well, you picked him."

I had no frame of reference for what I was about to experience. Instead, during my MBA studies, which I had just completed, the course had taken considerable time focusing on how the most influential organizations eliminated unproductive thinking and practices. A book that influenced my thinking and that I endeavored to practice was Peter Senge's *The Fifth Discipline*. Senge laid out a strong case that the most competitive and productive organizations adopted learning organizations' strategies. They were moving into the future through continual learning. By becoming a "learning organization," everyone becomes a participant in the organization's growth. It was a vision of work that I had embraced and planned on implementing in the IT department. What affected my thinking the most in Senge's book, and what played a role in helping me deal with the onslaught of Byzantine thinking was Senge's first of his five disciplines, personal mastery. I had never thought of personal mastery in terms of discipline. It's an essential one for a successful career and a meaningful life. Senge equates it with personal growth and learning of those who "are continually expanding their ability to create the life results they truly seek."

What I sought for my department was that we'd become a strategic partner in the entire organization's success. I was open to learning and growing, as were many of those I worked with. With that frame of reference in mind, I took Wayne's charge to nominate someone from the corporate staff we could work with as a new opening, an opportunity to have a direct channel to the executive suite and a more significant influence of the growth dynamic of the PUD.

So, when I gathered the supervisors together to discuss Wayne's new charge to nominate a new manager, we did so with anticipation that something good was about to happen. Since it was made clear to us that no one from IT would be considered for this role we had to identify someone that we believed could be a partner to help advance our initiatives. After much discussion, we settled on a man who had on occasion spoken positively about our department, someone we thought might advocate for our role within the organization. With the rapid changes in our industry, we needed someone with an open mind to raise our concerns to the highest levels.

We submitted the name of Steve Currit to Wayne with the sense we'd made a good choice.

It wasn't long before Steve came to our department and settled into his new role. He had no direct IT experience. He had spent most of his tenure in the real estate department. His only credentials for his new post, as it would come to light, was his relationship with Charlie Hosken, who had moved him from position to position because he had "plateaued." To me, that meant he had reached a dead-end in his career and either was no longer useful in his current position, or he wasn't eligible for a promotion. Whatever the reason, Charlie had plucked him out of his previous job and needed a slot for him. And that's how he came to oversee the IT department.

That I would report to a man whose IT knowledge was limited to turning on his PC on his desk was a reality I had to deal with. I adjusted my attitude very quickly and sought to bring him into the circle of our concerns. But that wasn't his game plan from the first day he settled into his new office.

In one of our first meetings, it was evident he was sent to stir things up—a trademark Hosken tactic. He explained that the new team Roger Braden and Charlie Hosken had alluded to at the Port Ludlow retreat the previous year had been formalized. Their task was to implement an enterprise software system that would effectively integrate all the PUD's data into one connected system.

While the prospect of new systems excited me, I was also concerned about why new technology was being considered without my department's input. No one had asked for help from my staff of very experienced professionals. It wouldn't take long after Steve arrived for the sinking feeling to set in that Hosken had set us up.

After he announced the team's formation, Steve said we were going to conduct an IT strategy exercise. The purpose would be to recommend a new direction for the IT department going forward. I showed him the work we'd already done on that issue, but he wasn't interested. We were to write a Request for Proposal (RFP) and solicit bids for the new evaluation. The plan was to use the consultant's report to present to the commissioners to justify the software's purchase. At this point, I didn't know what enterprise software the new team had in mind since none of us in IT had any conversations with the new group.

Before I left his office that day, he said something that

completely floored me. I was to immediately curtail all my peer associations—internally as well as externally. When I tried to explain the value of those industry relationships to the PUD, he didn't want to hear any of it. He matter-of-factly stated that I would need to put all my energies into managing my staff during the project. To say I was stunned would be an understatement. He also canceled my travel budget.

By the time I got back to my office, I was seething. All the time and effort I'd invested in communicating within our organization. All the time and energy I'd spent networking with other utilities nationwide, which had brought tremendous value to our organization. Trade associations such as American Public Power Association and Northwest Public Power were educational opportunities. And now I was to drop those relationships. What spoke to the intentions of management was that no one was to replace me. Whoever had decided to cut my wings was also intent on diminishing the entire department's role, a vicious slap across the face of a lot of dedicated and hardworking people.

Sitting behind my desk reflecting on what had just happened, I knew things were going to get more challenging for me. Hosken had announced this project last year at the Port Ludlow retreat, but I hadn't heard a word more about it until just now. Hosken wanted this project and intended to push it forward at all costs. From what I gathered from my meeting with Steve, I seemed to be in their way.

When I announced to my peers that I would no longer attend the monthly meetings, my fellow directors became wary of me. They thought I didn't want to participate any longer, even though I expressed that I had been directed not to attend. Since no one from IT attended either, it isolated my department from the rest of the organization. Reflecting on it, I'm confident the reasoning behind having me drop out of the internal directors' meeting was to tarnish my reputation within the company as a team player.

Had this been Hosken's intentions all along? I felt certain Steve arrived with marching orders straight from the top. Was Hosken seeking to infuriate me until I stormed off in anger?

Whatever the motivation, isolating me from my industry peers and diminishing my role within the company confused and upset me. But I knew I had to get a grip on my emotions. I had seen others in similar situations. They had become so embittered by their perceived persecution they lost their effectiveness as managers and employees. This negative attitude spilled over into their lives away from work, turning their very existence into a mess. I knew this would happen to me—if I let it. So, I asked myself one day, "Is this the way I want to go forward in my life?" Once I allowed my attitude to slip, I knew that work would become drudgery and boring, justifying management's further actions. Hosken had already forced key employees at my level out after falling into disfavor with him. A growing number of managers and supervisors had begun to challenge Hosken's management practices and to try to get him to recognize the destructive effects of his actions. Most had suffered his wrath in one form or another.

We were reluctant but principled and resolute members of a brotherhood. Save for the degree to which the community ascribed to us, we never allowed ourselves to descend into victim hood. In spite of the economic upheaval, alienation from our friends and families, interruption in our careers and near criminal mistreatment, we still maintained a culture of honor. Perhaps more accurately, we were an "intrepid brotherhood" because we had the fortitude to stand up to what we recognized as a destructive force. In all, there were probably close to ten of us, perhaps more if you consider people like John Beatty. In retrospect, we were probably fortunate to escape without submitting to the conditioning that would have made us ineffective anywhere else. None of us chose to be part of the brotherhood. In my case, I'd worked too hard and come too far to be shoved aside. I refused to become an easy target for him.

The first principle of Senge's book *The Fifth Discipline*, "personal mastery," came to mind. If I wanted to have a positive outcome, which I did, even in this hostile atmosphere, I had to assess how I was approaching these events. Unless I fully committed to doing my personal best, I would not improve the situation I found myself in. I would have no sway in creating positive solutions if I didn't master myself. I realize this was a career-defining moment for me—it would also help shape what kind of manager and person I would become. If I gave in to anger and bitterness, everything I had worked for would be lost. So, I pushed myself to consider a rational approach to my situation.

At first, I tried to square my thinking to Steve's rationale for his decisions—I would need all my energy to focus on this new project that was so vital to the company's future. We were to procure a consultant who would write a report that would look very much like it came out of the IT department since we would be writing the RFP and have a significant assay, or so I thought, in choosing the consultant to perform it. The report would also be used to justify to the commissioners purchasing an expensive piece of software and implementing the enterprise project. While it sounded plausible, it's what happened next that convinced me otherwise.

Steve began piling on me an unusual amount of work. He assigned me more work day by day than one person could reasonably get done within his deadlines. At this point, I knew they were trying to force me to leave. When I didn't meet the short deadlines, I'm sure he planned to document my failures. This documentation would find its way to a personnel file he was keeping. An obvious ploy that in time became apparent to the entire IT staff.

It was only natural that I was angry. Currit expected me to react because the work he assigned me was too voluminous and had no purpose other than a personal attack on me. As upset as I was at the underhandedness of the whole affair, I found ways to keep my emotions in check. I would go home and talk about it with Deanna. She understood the stress I was under and listened sympathetically. Finding strength at home, I chose not to let management's strategies succeed. I had no intention of succumbing to their games. I knew that Steve wouldn't do something like this on his own. He was following orders, and probably had learned well from the master manipulator himself, Charlie Hosken.

Here was another opportunity to keep focused on my goals, practice personal mastery, and not let this petty way of operating force me to get off track. I was determined to meet every deadline, so I began delegating much of the work. As an organization, we got so much work done—we met every deadline. This had several effects. The first was that my coworkers became aware of what I was going through personally. This wasn't a standard set of work requests for our department, and some of the tasks had little bearing on our operation. Second, everyone saw Steve for what he was: a total jerk—a sycophant carrying dirty water for a mendacious and possibly sociopathic leader.

One day, I was in my office meeting with a consultant we'd worked with for years when Steve walked in. I cordially introduced the man and told Steve that his consulting work had brought great value to the PUD, and he had just stopped by to follow up with us.

Steve turned to him and, with the rudest tone, told him he'd no longer be working with me. From now on, Steve was his only contact in the IT department. He told him not to contact me again.

I was shocked at his brusqueness. My face flushed, but I held my tongue. I was hurt, yes, but I was deeply embarrassed for Steve. He'd made a complete ass of himself. The consultant wasn't stupid. He understood what was going on. So did I. Another Hosken intimidation tactic.

The next day Steve took my private office away and assigned me to a cubicle.

The aggressive workload went on for the next three months. Staff would corner me in the break room or a hallway and ask me what was going on. During IT staff meetings, they were straightforward. "Are they trying to push you out?" they would ask. What was behind all the harassment? They saw through what management was trying to pull off. I feared losing them to bitterness and defeat. Keeping the workforce positive and pointed in the right direction was vital to me. I emphasized with them that we needed to keep working diligently on all our responsibilities. The quality of our work would speak for us.

We completed the RFP for the IT review we'd been tasked to prepare and began soliciting bids. Before that contract was awarded, several things took place.

With the increased workload and my fellow workers always on edge, I had to do something. At that time, I didn't know what they were doing was called "constructive discharge," but I didn't have to know the legal name to know it was a distasteful and probably an illegal strategy. But thanks to the cooperation of the IT staff, we had met all the deadlines. I feared if this workload went on much longer, there would be a rebellion. I knew I had to confront Steve.

About three months into their campaign of humiliation, I decided it was time for me to have a frank discussion with Steve. I believe in being direct, and in his office one day I came right out and stated: "I perceive that you're trying to give me too much work to do so you can create a personnel file to document my shortcomings so you can terminate me." He wasn't used to people calling him out. He honestly thought that I couldn't figure out his plan or bring it to his attention. Or that I wouldn't have the guts to speak up. I'm not sure which, but as I spoke, I could see the bile rising within him. He became visibly angry as if I had no right to question him. Was he ashamed of his tactics or of being put on the spot?

He finally responded, "Just keep your head down and get the work done."

Our meeting was over. But now, we both knew where we stood. I knew his plan, and he knew I knew. But I always maintained a flicker of hope that his petty tactics would cease, and we could get back to operating on an honest basis.

Currit's attitude toward me didn't change, and that didn't go unnoticed.

The other reaction came from the entire IT staff, many of them expressing their dissatisfaction with the workload, how I was being treated, and the department's low morale since Steve took over.

Again, I went to Steve and laid out all the staff's concerns. His reply was classic. He asked me to ask them what tools they needed to make their jobs easier. He didn't intend to change his behavior because that would admit defeat.

I approached the staff with Steve's request. One person noted that it sounded like he was trying to buy the department off with new tools. I agreed—it did sound that way. I instead redirected them to the opportunity to have better tools. Not that I expected a bunch of new toys to change their attitude toward an obnoxious manager, but it would help them to be more efficient in their daily routines. They agreed and gave me a long list of equipment requests, including new laptops and communications devices. Steve, to his credit, got the budget and supplied the requested equipment. But it didn't change the staff's concerns about the way the IT department, in general, was being treated, and me in particular. Eventually, that dissatisfaction would lead to an effort to organize the department under a union.

Meanwhile, remember the RFP for the IT evaluation was completed and published, and we began accepting proposals. You will recall, this review of the company's IT function was the initial deliverable of the new Enterprise Technology Solutions director. A wide range of companies responded—small, regional, and national firms submitted bids. We began to evaluate them based on their merits: price, performance, reputation, and other factors. This was a months-long process, but in mid-2001, the project committee, with IT staff participation, recommended a reputable consultant who had extensive expertise in the type of evaluation we required. Not surprisingly, we were overruled by Steve Currit and the bosses he answered to. A single consultant shop run by a fellow named Bob Fuller was chosen. We had rated his proposal way down on the list of viable candidates. But that didn't matter to the ultimate decision-makers. As it turned out, Bob Fuller had a long history with Hosken—they had been colleagues at Deloitte & Touche.

I was always trying to look on the bright side of a situation. I expected Bob Fuller to take an objective look at our department, just as the Navigant consultant had done two years before. Maybe Hosken would stop his hostile takedown of IT when he saw things were in order. Of course, that was too much to expect. Bob Fuller spent all of an hour in IT, mainly talking to the software development team. He did nothing more than wave to me as he passed by my cubicle. We did not learn until much later that in his acceptance letter to Steve Currit following the award of the bid, Mr. Fuller acknowledged the conditions under which this exercise was to be conducted, stating, "I understand this study is to be conducted with participation from the (enterprise) project team and the focus team." The focus team was comprised of employees from departments who used IT services. There is no mention of collaborating with or interviewing IT personnel.

Fuller spent all his time with the new project team, drafting their definition of the PUD's future IT requirements. Ironically, much of his final report was useful to our department. Predictably, it included a list of areas that could be improved or upgraded that would benefit the organization. It was remarkable, however, that these recommendations were presented as new. In reality, all of them had been formally suggested to management multiple times before this new project was even envisioned.

He was given instructions not to talk to me in his information gathering for an obvious reason. If I had the opportunity to show him our past initiatives or the Navigant performance review, his report would have been unnecessary. The purpose of that maneuver was to make it appear that I had not done my job by failing to propose these improvement initiatives. The report was as much a condemnation of my department and me individually as it was a future strategy. It is also important to note that three years later, in April 2004, we conducted an unofficial audit of the recommendations in Fuller's strategy report. Not surprisingly, the only thing that had been accomplished was the progress-to-date on the enterprise software project. None of the other recommendations had even been discussed. Further evidence that the exercise was conducted only to justify the pet project of the manager and to cast the existing IT department in an unfavorable light.

It was true that most of our software systems had reached legacy status. They needed upgrading or replacing. Our department already had plans formulated to convert existing software systems to new hardware platforms or to extend the life of existing systems by changing database systems and transitioning to new programming languages. But Fuller and the enterprise software team ultimately recommended a sophisticated enterprise system. Charlie Hosken now had what he wanted most: a professional opinion, in writing, that would push him a step forward toward acquiring his massive enterprise project.

This was the straw that broke the camel's back for some of my staff. The department's Applications Development Manager, Doug Stewart, was a gifted IT professional, and he knew his job well. He came to my cubicle and asked to be reassigned. He was upset at how I was being treated and how the project was being handled. Working with Steve Currit was something he didn't want to do any longer. He had astutely detected that Charlie's reign as manager would include many patronage appointments and quid-pro-quo contract awards. Currit's appointment to run a department that he had no professional experience in was a good example of that. Doug decided to wash his hands of the entire project and resign as a supervisor subject to Steve Currit's direction. Doug's decision was a real blow to the new program just getting underway. Especially since Doug was best qualified to address the software needs and to write the specs. I convinced Steve to carve out a new position for Doug as Chief Software Architect, since we needed his expertise.

Under Bob Fuller's guidance, the project team was tasked to write another RFP for an enterprise system. The requirements definition process was exhaustive and impressive, providing a comprehensive set of evaluation criteria for the proposals that would be submitted. The RFP was published, and proposals were received in mid-2001. The team received several "Tier One" proposals from companies like PeopleSoft, Oracle, and J.D. Edwards and some from "Tier Two" companies like National Information Solutions Cooperative. After initial evaluations and scripted demonstrations, the team narrowed the list to three Tier One companies: PeopleSoft, Oracle, and J.D. Edwards. Things had started to change to a degree by this time. Management realized that a critical resource for the success of their project, namely the IT staff, was extremely dissatisfied with how they and I were being treated. Mr. Currit "changed his spots" to a degree to keep the IT staff engaged. He restored some of my travel budget and stopped piling tasks on my shoulders that were impossible to accomplish. The project team allowed me to participate in visits to other utilities to assess their enterprise software projects. Although I was not acknowledged as a project team member, and I had to cover the travel from my own budget rather than project funds.

Ultimately, the system that best met all the needs of the RFP was PeopleSoft, and with all its proposed modules was a massive program that exceeded our requirements. Our department perspective was that everything in the Tier One level was overkill for Chelan County PUD. We were allowed to participate during the "scripted demos" and on-site presentations by the vendors, and we took care to make it clear that Tier Two systems like NISC met most, if not all, of the requirements at a fraction of the cost. Once PeopleSoft was chosen (over our objections) we were limited to trying to suggest elimination of some of the proposed modules in order to reduce cost, and purchasing insurance against someone taking over PeopleSoft and orphaning the system. This was a concern because large, enterprise level software companies were "licking their chops" to devour the customer bases of their competitors. Takeovers and consolidations were happening right and left. For instance, just in the time frame of our own project, Oracle would take over J.D. Edwards and acquire SPL Worldgroup (the company that wrote PeopleSoft's customer information and billing system). They were also making overtures toward acquisition of PeopleSoft and, although industry experts doubted that would happen, insurance against someone acquiring the company and forcing customers to convert to the products of the acquiring entity might be a reasonable precaution.

But nothing we said mattered. Hosken presented the findings of his EBS team to the commissioners. In September 2002, the commissioners approved a $1.28 million contract with PeopleSoft to provide a 42-module software system, with estimated future costs to reach a total of $6 million, with a total project estimate (including implementation) of $8.5 million. As it turned out, this was a low-ball projection. The EBS team would return again and again for more money as the program ultimately ran out of control.

To this day, what fills me with questions every time I think about it is, what were the commissioners thinking? Admittedly, there was no one on the EBS team with technology experience or even experience in IT projects, and we were expressly forbidden to converse with the commissioners or any one on the IT steering committee about the project without EBS personnel present. Still, none of them asked any hard questions or wanted to know what the IT department thought about this proposal. Not one of them asked about future costs. Not one of them wondered why a company with 600 employees needed such a robust enterprise system with 42-modules that would be sufficient to meet the Pentagon's worldwide needs. None of them asked if $6 million would be the absolute top-end cost for the project? No one on the EBS team knew the answer to that. Yet, the commissioners approved the outlay in one meeting, with one brief discussion. These were all elected commissioners who had campaigned to sit on the board with promises to oversee the significant financial decisions. Yet, in this case, it appeared their vote was nothing more than a rubber stamp. Did Charlie Hosken have some magical powers over them so they simply did his bidding? This is something we will never know. I know that if those with the fiduciary responsibilities of oversight failed to ask the right questions, which led the PUD into a financial and operational quagmire, it was the ability to ask the right questions that led certain ones to the truth.

Shortly after Doug's resignation as Applications Development Supervisor in late 2001, we began the process to replace him.

We interviewed several candidates, and one fit the bill of what we needed. Mark Bolz was highly qualified—an ex-Marine officer, trained in systems and software management at the Perot Systems Corporation, he had all the qualifications and more the EBS project needed. Steve and Jeff Smith, the EBS Project Manager, met with him separately and agreed he was the one.

I was asked to express my opinion on his technical expertise, and I was well satisfied he would be a real asset not only to the EBS project, but also to the IT department in general. He came aboard in March 2002 and was immediately "gobbled up" by the EBS team to participate as a significant part of their project.

Mark brought an interesting dynamic to the department. Besides his undeniable talent and training as a software applications engineer, he also had a sense of ethics that made him stand out. He knew how to read people, to dig beneath appearances to the rock bottom truth. His acumen with large systems came from his training with Ross Perot and his Perot Systems after his military service. At Perot, he had worked with large corporations with thousands of employees, organizations that benefited from expansive enterprise systems. I very soon realized that he was the perfect candidate to replace Doug as the supervisor of the analysts and developers. In April, we placed him in charge of Doug's former staff.

Mark understood how to develop applications for specific purposes, and in the short time he worked with Jeff Smith, Steve Currit, and the EBS team across the street, he saw right through them. After less than six months on the EBS project, he sought me out to have a private conversation.

He asked if we could have a frank conversation about his job, my job, and the EBS team in general. Mark was a careful observer, both of the EBS team and in the department offices with the IT staff. When he was hired, he'd been left with the impression that he was needed for the EBS project because I wasn't qualified to work on it myself. But after witnessing my leadership in the department, how we operated, the quality of our work, along with the sophistication of our current systems, he concluded he'd been lied to. He also had significant reservations about the EBS team itself. It was composed of individuals with no IT experience or knowledge, and the system they were purchasing and implementing would be a colossal waste of money. It was far too large for the needs of the organization, and the decisions being made by the inexperienced team were not cost-effective. In short order, Mark had put his finger on the pulse of the problem. The group itself wasn't qualified to perform what they'd been tasked to accomplish. Mark feared that once this project failed due to its leaders' incompetence, the blame would roll down to him, the department, and ultimately to me.

I appreciated his comments, as these were my fears too. What he told me next confirmed my feelings and what others in the department had been sensing. Mark related a conversation he had with Jeff Smith and Steve Currit about my position. They both intimated that I wouldn't be with the PUD much longer, and if he played his cards right, the director's job could be his. As a result, Mark wanted no part in the underhanded tactics and had asked to step away from the EBS team and be reassigned to work full-time in the IT department.

So here we were—the program had barely begun, and we were in the process of choosing an implementation partner. Not one but two seasoned and talented IT professionals had backed out of working directly with the hand-picked EBS team. I hoped the message these professionals were sending would alter Steve and Jeff's attitudes and alert them that they were flailing blindly in a Sisyphean endeavor.

When I explained Mark's request to Steve, he sighed deeply. I was hoping that Steve was astute enough to understand the ramifications of two highly respected IT professionals withdrawing from the project. I wanted to believe that it would force a moment of introspection—maybe he would ask himself why these highly qualified men didn't want to work with him and his team. If he asked the right questions, he could get to the truth of what he was up against in trying to shoehorn this gargantuan software program into our much smaller operation. What would it take for him to ask if there was any truth to Doug and Mark's fears? I could see it in his eyes that whatever it would take, he didn't have it. If he did ask himself such questions, in the back of his mind, he only saw that sword of Damocles hanging over his head by a very thin thread—if he didn't do his job, it wouldn't take but a twitch of the puffy fingers of the manipulator upstairs to snap that thread.

These interactions with Steve and Hosken and others of his ilk had left their marks on me. I have learned from them as much as I have learned from the best of managers. I have observed there are two primary management styles. Those who want to know the facts as they are, and those who come to a task with their ready-made illusions and are determined to press their version of reality on everyone else.

The objective leaders don't come to the table with preconceived notions of how to solve a problem but are willing to hold off judgment so they can ascertain the truth of the situation— they want to hear and see the facts, the details, the opinions of those who are doing the work, those in the field. They have the emotional intelligence to put themselves in the shoes of those performing the tasks. They want the best remedy for everyone concerned because their agenda is to create a better organization—one that is more productive, more responsive to customers' needs. They want everyone under them to grow with them, to benefit from the fruits of their mutual labors.

These were the managers I worked under at the PUD earlier in my career. They didn't fear asking the tough questions, and they didn't fear being asked tough questions because they didn't fear the truth. Leaders like this admire and encourage critical thinking skills in their colleagues because most creative solutions to problems come from the people on the front lines. Critical thinking destroys illusions and reaches down to the bedrock. And organizations built on a bedrock of best practices and ethical leadership can withstand the test of hard times.

The second type of leader is the illusion maker who creates their own reality. The illusion serves their private purposes, whatever those purposes happen to be: more power, control, wealth, and ultimately to preserve their version of reality as they perceive it. Since their reality doesn't conform to the facts of the situation, they don't ask any questions of anyone who would disturb their version of the truth. Anyone who wants to stay in favor with the illusion makers must give up their critical thinking skills. Those who offer constructive solutions, or ask questions contrary to their orthodox thinking, are pushed out the door or otherwise sidelined. Under the guise of reforming the status quo, they create a new status quo in which they can operate freely. The facts on the ground matter little to these leaders and their followers—they will shape the facts to conform to their reality.

Charlie Hosken was a master at creating problems where they didn't exist. This was the illusion he created about himself as a problem solver and innovator. He then could swoop in and save the organization from the old-timers running it into the ground. He was steadily pushing out anyone who dared to question his view of reality.

Steve was a perfect Hosken disciple. He couldn't see issues through others' eyes, let alone listen to the experts around him who tried to tell him the grand project he was involved with had severe problems. He had little ability that I could determine to do any deep reflection, to make connections, to see the entire picture, or to connect emotionally with anyone outside his circle. Critical thinking and emotional intelligence weren't required for his position. He bought into Hosken's delusion of saving the PUD, and there was little I could do to dissuade him.

When Steve and I discussed Mark leaving the EBS team, he looked up at me and said, "You're the only one qualified to replace him. So, you're it."

The decision was made. I moved across the street to the headquarters of the EBS team and was assigned an office. From this moment forward, Steve's direct mistreatment stopped. Now that he needed my expertise to help salvage the program, he could tolerate my presence. I still maintained my responsibilities of running the IT department, but I had a lot of help from a great staff. I didn't look forward to my new assignment, but I was prepared to do my absolute best to make it a success. But it did create some anxiety in me—what would I be running into that two of my most experienced colleagues couldn't handle? I would find that out soon enough.

Despite my best efforts, I couldn't help but bring the tension of my work home with me. I didn't want to upset Deanna. I knew my problems at work caused her concern, too. Would I lose my job? Would we have to move away from the area? Our kids were raised here in the Wenatchee area. Not only our kids, but our grandkids, and our roots were here. And the ultimate question that concerned both of us: Would we be able to retire?

Our conversations weren't all about our worries. She was a generous support to me and believed, as I did, that I should stick it out. Things could change in a heartbeat. I'd put in too many years here to just walk away. Somewhere, somehow, someone with clout would catch Charlie in a lie and put an end to his tenure.

At home, Deanna and I went about our lives. She trusted me and knew I was doing my absolute best at work. We stayed positive by engaging in our regular schedule, visiting our kids and friends, traveling on weekends, and shopping together as we've done for years.

One day at Costco, we were in one of the aisles of tall merchandise picking up things when I noticed Steve down the way. I pushed our cart up to him, offering a greeting.

"Hello, Steve."

He looked up a bit suspiciously.

"This is my wife, Deanna," I said. "This is Steve Currit." I wanted to introduce her since I talked about him so much. He stood staring, speechless for a long pause.

"Oh, hi," he stumbled. "Gordon is doing real well."

It didn't surprise me he couldn't even offer a friendly greeting or engage in small talk. Instead, he sounded like an elementary school teacher offering an impromptu report on a student. He sounded so immature that I wanted to laugh.

"Of course he's doing well," Deanna said, not at all caught off guard. "He's the best person you have in IT."

He mumbled something, glanced at her, then me, and skulked off down the row. I don't want to mischaracterize him, but he did look like a weasel, bent over, trying to find a dark hole to crawl into. Standing here talking to us would be too difficult for his fragile ego. I turned and kissed Deanna. We went about our day, happy to have one another and confident in ourselves that we were living true to our values—we had not one thing to hang our heads over. With Deanna's coolness and assurance backing me, I believed I could endure just about anything Steve threw at me. As it turned out, I would need every bit of that confidence for what I endured over the next two years.

CHAPTER 4

The Bloom Is Off The Rose

As I set up my office across the street close to the EBS team, I had some time to catch up on the situation. Mark had blown through the team and its efforts like a cyclone, tearing into them for the software they chose and the amount of software they had purchased. He believed they had needlessly purchased a system that wasn't appropriate for the PUD. He didn't take their lack of experience in IT lightly.

Though the EBS team was competent in their areas of expertise, they willingly took on an endeavor beyond their scope of training and experience. And he had little patience with incompetence and even less with arrogant people he believed weren't taking his input seriously. Mark had immediately picked up on the culture of what he called "entitlement." Hosken had anointed them with this task of revolutionizing the PUD and its information systems, a task they took seriously but didn't have the experience to avoid technical missteps.

I knew what I was up against, but I was determined to do my absolute best to make the project successful. As I began to participate in the meetings, the two issues Mark had brought to my attention became front and center concerns. They had to be solved quickly for the project to make any appreciable move forward. Though I was slighted at almost every turn, my goal was to do everything I could to save the project. I believed then, as I do to this day, that if the leadership group had been more open to input from the IT professionals earlier on, the implementation nightmare that would break out into a public embarrassment in the months ahead could have been avoided— entirely. Any failure to implement the comprehensive program in the months ahead would not be due to a lack of competence on any individual's part but to an overall superior attitude that didn't allow them to listen to common sense.

I lay the blame for the superior attitude of the EBS team at the feet of Charlie Hosken and his puerile efforts to exercise control and authority over every aspect of the PUD's operation. It became apparent to me early on that someone had shaped their thinking to the point that they believed that IT wasn't an essential function that required any specialized training. Hosken was out to prove any warm body could be plucked from nearly any department to oversee the organization's vital information and technical functions. That philosophy brought a real estate man to manage the IT department and a former radio announcer to run the EBS team itself.

There were many fine details of the acquisition that had been overlooked, details that would have a broad impact on the entire operation. Details that could have been ironed out earlier if a qualified IT professional had been consulted. Mark pointed out the most nettlesome issue was the purchase of the PeopleSoft enterprise system itself—he considered it risky. They were the smallest player in Tier One enterprise systems. Mark tried to explain that industry consolidation happens quite regularly, and by purchasing from the smallest player, they were setting themselves up. If a competitor acquired PeopleSoft, support would be terminated, making their system obsolete. Buying from Oracle or SAP would be a safer long-term bet, as would purchasing from a lower-tier provider. Mark was laughed at by ERP team members. As if it were a prophecy, these very events took place over the next decade, but that is not the central part of our story.

Doug Stewart, a senior member of the IT staff, was prescient in his analysis that most people wanted a modern experience with financial data. Doug incessantly pushed back on the contention that our existing systems were obsolete or "end-of-life." He documented the reality that there were reasonable solutions available to upgrade existing software to meet most of the requirements used to select a new enterprise system. This alternative would significantly modernize the reports and data sent out to the departments at a fraction of the cost.

All these observations were taken as criticism and dismissed by the ERP managers. They wanted the robust PeopleSoft system for reasons that contradicted the facts on the ground. This decision was only the beginning of the problems that would surface over the next couple of years.

When I joined the EBS team meetings, I immediately sensed the tension between the team members and any input from the IT team. They took up a defensive posture, a circle-the-wagons attitude to protect themselves from outside criticism. So, when I began to present solutions to the apparent dilemmas that had to be solved, they were reluctant to listen.

When I began attending the meetings, my immediate concern was to resolve the problems Mark had raised regarding deficiencies in the contract the EBS team had negotiated with PeopleSoft. When Bob Fuller wrote the RFP for the enterprise system, he didn't require bidders to perform a hardware assessment. Typically, a hardware evaluation is included to determining the funds necessary to upgrade the current equipment. So there were minimal funds in the contract to upgrade the PUD's computer systems. The first step was a competent assessment of the PUD's current technology and what it would need to upgrade for the new software's proper operation. With all its 42 modules, the size of the program would not operate efficiently, if at all, on our current equipment, an embarrassing oversight for the EBS team.

When Mark pointed it out, it angered the team members, as if he had doubted their competence. They had been caught with egg on their face by department personnel who they were determined weren't capable of helping them. The superior attitude of the EBS team members became one of the biggest hurdles to a smooth implementation. They just didn't want to listen to me or anyone from my department unless I brought in experts from the outside to confirm what I was saying was accurate. This attitude of mistrust from the very beginning created a profoundly flawed working relationship between the two teams—EBS and IT. Even though we were situated only across the street from each other, it was as if we were on different planets. The EBS team, as well-meaning as they were, had descended from Planet Hosken, where they freely breathed in his delusional thinking. Most of my staff was housed in the PUD headquarters and worked with their feet solidly on the ground. We serviced all the departments' needs and strove to implement the industry's best practices in our operations.

This divide between the two operations was an artificial creation and didn't have to happen, but it was the reality I stepped into in early 2002.

My first order of business was to resolve the significant obstacle to beginning the implementation. Since the EBS team balked at Mark's demand for a technical assessment, I persuaded the team to have a conference call with a Hewlett-Packard engineer (all our hardware was HP), who agreed a hardware assessment was required. They would have a company representative come out and perform it. Eventually, the EBS team leaders approached the commissioners for an additional $1.6 million to acquire what we needed. This was not the last time the team leaders would trundle back into the commissioner's meetings, hands out, asking for more money. Their request was dutifully funded, equipment was ordered, and we installed it. We were then ready for the next step.

The next issue that had to be solved quickly was the multiple versions of development tools. Because the different modules were written in different versions of the PeopleSoft "programming language," installing them as they were delivered would require retaining and using the two different sets of tools to maintain the system. Again, it was difficult to convince the

EBS team of the complexity this problem would create. They treated my concerns with disdain. Only after I orchestrated another conference call with PeopleSoft were they willing to accept the solution. All modules would be upgraded to the most current programming language, obviating the need to have dual sets of development tools.

Perhaps the most significant example of our "save-your-bacon" approach to our tormentors was what we called the SETID issue. The centerpiece of the business systems at most utilities is the customer information and billing system. PeopleSoft did not have its own billing system. They had purchased a product from a company called SPL WorldGroup that converted it with their software tools to fit with the rest of the PeopleSoft system. I will discuss later how Oracle acquired PeopleSoft and then bought SPL WorldGroup in the 2004 to 2006 timeframe. If you are paying attention, you have already picked up that this is a prime example of Tier One Enterprise System acquisition and compression, the very thing that Mark had warned the EBS team about. In a nutshell, the PeopleSoft financial systems identified "customers" with a particular label in their database structure. Everywhere a customer record of any kind existed in the PeopleSoft financial systems, a customer was referred to with this label. That way, you could be assured of finding everything related to a particular customer by merely using their identification value (customer number) in this one field (referred to in the database as a SETID). However, the SPL WorldGroup customer information and billing system used a different label or SETID to record the customer number. So, even though the customer had one number or ID, it would not be possible to find every record for that customer across the entire system because the two databases had different fields to record the customer number.

The upshot is that the enterprise system that Charlie Hosken envisioned that would allow information to be shared across the entire organization would have fallen far short of that goal if it had been implemented as it had been delivered.

My staff made the formal case to the project team to standardize the database labels for customer ID across the entire system to accomplish this fundamental objective. There was a minimal additional cost associated with making this change. Eventually, we prevailed, and the databases were changed to reflect the standardization objective. Once again, our professionalism prevented delay and embarrassment, but we received no acknowledgment or gratitude.

≋⫮≋

Over the next two years, my job was to put out fires, solve problems, and work as a liaison between the EBS team and what they thought they could accomplish and the IT team who understood the reality on the ground. My role in the PeopleSoft project was to participate as a member of the core team and assume tasks only the IT staff could resolve. My primary focus, my mantra, was to keep my staff focused on the project to ensure that they met their responsibilities. My training, education, and background told me that we needed to meet our responsibilities and expectations or put the project at risk. My primary admonition to my staff was to "keep your heads down, get your work done, and meet expectations. We need to do this to make it successful for the company and ourselves." All of this had to be executed in an environment where everyone in charge was trying to exclude me and diminish my role as much as possible. They had an ulterior motive and objective for treating me this way. It would not become evident to me what their plans were until sometime later. What was apparent was that everyone on the EBS team, from the director down to the administrative assistant, had been given the direction and dispensation to ignore me, criticize me, embarrass me, and to generally treat me like dirt.

In January 2003, commissioners approved another contract for an implementation partner. The $3.9 million award went to a highly respected technology company that had experience in the public sector. I will refer to them going forward as the "contractor." Since no one from my department was involved in negotiating the contract, I wasn't aware of the terms. But I had every reason to assume this implementation would proceed smoothly.

In a typical implementation, the contractor works under the direction of a department IT manager. In addition to me, there were some very experienced and talented project managers in the IT department. Among them, Doug Stewart and Mark Bolz. In turn, the contractor would assign an experienced project manager who would manage their employees. I assumed they would work closely with my staff, who were highly accomplished and ready to work on the new project, despite their overall misgivings. I believe I had successfully pointed my team in the right direction, emphasizing that despite the EBS plan's flaws, it was our responsibility to conduct ourselves professionally and do what we could to make the project successful. I had every reason to believe that most of the EBS project goals could be accomplished if everyone worked together.

It's important here to define who we were, and how we responded to the mistreatment and discrimination from management and the EBS team. I have already mentioned how I had seen some of my peers in the industry become bitter and eventually given up on their careers when faced with a similar situation. My supervisors and I decided that would not be us. Although we knew the next few years would be a tremendous challenge, we drafted a plan to maintain employee morale while measuring continuous improvement and value to the company going forward. I arranged for a facilitated "visioning" exercise where we all participated in defining a mission and vision for the department. We designed and adopted a logo that we used on every department communication from that point forward. Our vision statement read "Information Technology: Active Partners in Business Technology Solutions/Collaboration with Purpose and Respect/Service Excellence."

We drafted a support plan for ourselves and the company that included sections on Striving for Quality, Communication, Building Morale, Improving Accessibility, Improving Attitudes, Improving Delivery, and Marketing/Image Activities. We took this plan very seriously and had measurement mechanisms in place to monitor our progress. Everyone coalesced around the plan.

At the end of 2002, we drafted an executive summary of our accomplishments and submitted it upward through the management chain. It began by stating that "Beginning in 2002, Information Technology focused on moving from being internally focused to becoming more client focused. We had a plan that involved developing a mission/vision statement, aligning our staff with our vision by providing training in IT service organization and consulting skills. We have focused on becoming confident rather than arrogant, embracing complaints, paying attention to moments of truth, and increasing our communication with clients."

The document went on to reveal that our department had realized the following improvements in customer satisfaction during the previous year:

- 44 percent increase in overall satisfaction
- 32 percent increase in timeliness of delivery satisfaction
- 27 percent increase in customer service satisfaction
- 51 percent increase in level of support satisfaction
- 23 percent increase in hardware and software satisfaction

Coincidentally, with the cooperation of the Corporate Communications Department and our internal print shop, we developed a poster that proclaimed our department successes and placed them at every entrance to the main headquarters building. It contained a long list of completed projects and service improvements, and my staff was proud to announce these to the world. These were tangible, documented benefits and improvements that provided significant value to the company. What we had realized is that there was a cultural revolution taking place in IT. What used to be considered "soft skills" were now core competencies that differentiated high performing IT organizations. Most Chief Information Officers were developing "human factors," not just technical skills, in their workforce.

Also, in the complete absence of any executive leadership, we took responsibility as a department to align our work efforts with the strategic objectives of the company. Most of the strategic planning efforts of the day were conducted using one or another of the popular framework methodologies. These tools gave companies a road map to define what was most important from a strategic perspective and then what was critically important to accomplish each strategic objective. Then, they could identify measurable indicators to help determine how they were doing in achieving those objectives. Any department head who was paying attention could use the strategic objectives and critical success factors as guideposts to determine what tactical projects were the most important for their respective departments to accomplish. We did this and used the results to evaluate and prioritize project requests to ensure we were applying our resources appropriately. However, since the utility had abandoned the ongoing information technology alignment function that we had established years earlier, there was no acknowledgment of our efforts or our process.

Our successes and discipline did not fit management's narrative. Our thanks was to find our posters ripped down and destroyed, and our summary of accomplishments suppressed and buried. Our fate was clear, but still we persevered.

≋◿≋

Within weeks of the contractor staff showing up in our department, problems began to arise. Doug Stewart regularly showed up in my office with concerns about the contracted individuals working on the project. He had a list of items they weren't completing. Mark also came to me, unhappy that the contracted staff were not meeting their assigned goals, yet the company was still getting paid according to their contract as if they were on schedule. This didn't sit well with the department staff.

In a separate conversation, I brought this up with Steve Currit, thinking he would want to see the contractor fulfill their contractual obligations. If he supported the staff's concerns, I was confident we could push forward. But that didn't happen. He told me that whatever the contractor didn't get done, the department had to complete. I was shocked, but not any more shocked than anything else that had come out of Steve's mouth. He was purposefully working at odds with the IT staff. I was continually left with the impression that he was out to prove something, some grand thesis that I wasn't privy to.

By May, the indecision and ineffectiveness of EBS management to monitor the large and complex implementation process had festered into a near revolt in my department. In his analytical and systematic manner, Doug wrote a long list of items yet to be completed, those not even begun, and the general failure of the contractor to perform. Mark was up in arms that incremental payments were still being made to the contractor despite their deficiencies even though key components would not be completed by them, such as the eApps for HR, Directory Services, and the PeopleSoft Enterprise Portal. All of these would fall on us to complete, even though the contractor was getting paid for the work.

Things boiled over when one of the contracted employees made it clear that Doug and the other PUD staff assigned to the implementation were to work under their direct supervision per the EBS managers' contract. Doug got visibly upset. He immediately came to my office to tell me what a contracted employee had just told him. Not only was the project falling behind, but this unorthodox arrangement, one that was not typical of any implementation engagement any of us had worked on, now had become even more complicated. The significant parts of the installation, such as Directory Services functionality, would be the sole responsibility of the IT staff. This struggle over who would actually do the work and bear ultimate responsibility for any unfinished work became a hot point of contention throughout the project. Before we leave this topic, consider that every member of the IT staff who was committed by agreement to support tasks in the EBS project were paid from my budget. Their fully-loaded salaries were being paid by Chelan County PUD. But, according to the agreement negotiated with the implementation partner, these same staff members were obligated to perform tasks that were in the scope of work for the contractor. So, just to connect the dots, the PUD was paying their own employees to function as contractor personnel. To put it mildly, it was a "head scratcher."

Mark and Doug compiled a memo of items that hadn't been completed and brought it to me. This document gained a life of its own and became referred to as the "May 19th memo," to be discussed in management and legal settings for the project's duration and well beyond. They wanted the memo pushed upstairs, directly to Joe Jarvis, assistant general manager for Finance and Technology, who was Steve Currit's boss. I told them the procedure was to take the memo first to my boss and to ask him to submit it to Mr. Jarvis. I knew if we took it directly to Mr. Jarvis, we would have hell to pay.

At my regular weekly meeting with Steve, I showed him the memo. I reiterated the men's concerns, emphasizing that these were the concerns of the entire staff working on the project. This implementation was falling behind. We would never meet our deadlines if the contractor didn't perform up to expectations.

Steve told me that he would discuss it with Mr. Jarvis. Additionally, he asked me to come up with a solution to handle the issues internally. In discussions with my staff, we decided on using an "issues log" where all their concerns would be recorded. Steve agreed and oversaw a weekly meeting to discuss the items to set priorities.

While at face value this seemed rational and reasonable to resolve the issues, these meetings changed nothing. Contracted staff was never asked to attend, which would have made the discussions much more productive. The hope was that the weekly sessions would establish a chain of accountability between the IT staff, EBS management, and the contracted project manager. But that wasn't how it worked. These meetings served no greater purpose than to ease Doug and Mark's concerns by listening. Steve had to tamp down the growing turmoil in the department over the lack of progress. He seemed more interested in keeping news of the trouble from seeping out of the confines of the department. By keeping Jarvis and the executive steering committee, composed of the commissioners and executive management, in the dark, he could continue to push for work to get done even as it fell further behind. Steve didn't show much concern for holding the contractor to account and pushed hard for Doug and Mark to find a way to get the needed work done.

While the meetings were held from May through October, defections and transfers from the EBS effort picked up substantially. PUD employees began voting with their feet.

Functional experts assigned to the EBS team asked to return to their respective departments. IT staff tasked with working on the PeopleSoft implementation requested reassignment, citing management's lack of support. Even the contracted project managers voluntarily moved on to other positions within their organization, creating churn in the contractor's onsite management.

Despite the weekly "issues log" meetings, nothing changed. Contractor staff assigned to the project weren't completing their agreed-upon tasks. Still, EBS management continued to authorize their payments, which continued to perplex Mark and Doug and the others working at full capacity trying to take up the slack.

That August, the first 16 programs were scheduled to be operational. But not one of them went live. With the missed deadlines, and the contractor dragging their feet, the tension in the department reached a breaking point. Steve refused to elevate our concerns, so the spotlight fell on my staff, not where it should have. The department's morale reached such a low point, out of fear for their careers, the team began talking to a union organizer.

Doug Stewart spearheaded it, inviting the International Brotherhood of Electrical Workers' representative to assist him in organizing a vote. Unionizing would put the workers in a protected class. The growing uncertainty in the department caused by the overbearing management style of the executives created a sense that everyone's job was at stake. The organizing process alone was an opportunity for team building and developing a greater understanding of their rights as employees. Once enough staff was on board, the IBEW representative made the necessary filings, and the process began. As a manager, I wasn't involved in any organizing meetings, but I understood Doug's and the others' concerns. There was a severe lack of communication outside of the department with the senior executives. Steve, evidently under orders from Hosken, had effectively isolated the department's staff.

It didn't surprise me that Doug took a leadership role in talking to his colleagues about the benefits of unionizing. Uncertainty and fear had to lurk in the back of everyone's minds, especially Doug's. He had been reprimanded by Steve Currit on several occasions, and had been subjected to counseling sessions after directly disputing statements made by project steering members in staff meetings. He also had communicated directly with steering committee members and legal counsel to further discussions that had taken place in meetings. Infuriated, Steve planned on disciplining Doug, but I objected.

If someone conducted a discipline session, it would be me since I was his direct superior. Besides, I told him, we need to address the concerns Doug raised in the meeting. An employee forum could clear the air. Steve brushed me off and called Doug in for a reprimand session.

Incredible as this all sounds, I can see that Steve's main job was to keep Steve looking good. If he could muzzle Doug by disciplining him, he had a better chance of keeping a lid on the department's brewing disaster. If the cat got out of the bag, there were problems with implementing the multi-million dollar, state-of-the-art enterprise system—one that would become obsolete in less than a decade—it would shoot up the chain of command, causing problems. Steve chaired the EBS steering committee comprised of the commissioners and executive management. He had formed this after relieving me of my responsibilities of attending the director's meetings, which established a communication channel between departments. With Steve on the steering committee, he could tell them what they wanted to hear.

When the news broke that the department personnel were seeking to organize, Steve cut off the issue log meetings, using the excuse that he wanted to show respect for the staff. I didn't believe that excuse for a moment. He was glad to have done with a regular meeting that had borne no appreciable results. The implementation was in disarray, and there was no systematic effort to address the concerns raised almost daily by the senior IT managers. At the first meeting with management to discuss the unionization in October 2003, held under the rules of the Public Employees Relations Commission, which forbade discussing contentious issues, Joe Jarvis expressed real anger at the IT department. As Jarvis spoke, it was evident he was in the dark about our concerns over the work, or lack of work, of the contractor. For his own reasons, which we'll never know, Steve had kept all the dissatisfaction in our department to himself. At one point, the conversation that day became heated, with Jarvis blaming the IT staff directly for trying to sabotage the PeopleSoft implementation. When Doug remonstrated and tried to inform Jarvis of the events leading up to their unionizing efforts, he refused to back off. He was convinced that if Doug, Mark, and the others wanted to complete the implementation, it would have already been finished. There was no mention of the contractor shortcomings.

Why Steve had not kept his superiors informed of the failure of the contractor to complete their contractual obligations, I can only surmise. As it turned out, the weekly issues meetings were nothing more than an exercise in futility, designed to appease the IT managers on the implementation's frontlines. No one held the contractor to account while Steve sat back and let things slide out of control. When Jarvis vocalized his accusation with such adamant force, Steve didn't offer one word of defense. He allowed the team he oversaw to take all the blame for events he well knew were out of the IT staff's control. Was this a weakness in his character or a deliberate attempt to destroy the IT department's cohesiveness? He's the only one that can answer that.

And what about Jarvis? He could have investigated earlier when the problems came to his attention. All the chaos could have been avoided—why Jarvis took the easy way out and spread the blame around like butter on bread instead of investigating the roots of the problems earlier is not a trivial question. It speaks to his effectiveness as a manager. Effective managers have their ears to the ground—they walk around and listen to their employees. They know what's going on. They don't let issues spin out of control. They are problem solvers. But that wasn't his style.

Maybe part of Jarvis's anger could be attributed to the unionizing efforts. Jarvis could have perceived Doug's organizing attempts as a slap across his face. Perhaps that's what Doug had in mind, to rattle their cage. It was the only way to make them listen. Communicating their concerns directly with upper management had proven fruitless. Why not try another method of poking the nest?

That fall, a series of employee forums were held with the executives to discuss the unionization efforts.

Contractor project managers came and went; some complained openly that this was the most challenging implementation they had ever experienced. More and more responsibility for completing the work fell on our IT staff, with less accountability for the contractor's failures.

By October, it was evident to someone in the executive team that changes had to be made. Steve Currit was told he'd be moved out of his position. It wasn't official until December that he would take up managing the PUD's parks department.

There was no love lost in Steve's exit—he didn't even stop into my office to say adios, he just disappeared. With his departure, I had hope that some sanity would return to our department. Unfortunately, that wasn't to be.

Because of increased visibility of the issues raised in the May 19th memo, as well as other turmoil surrounding the project, Joe Jarvis engaged RW Beck to review the EBS implementation. Even that effort was an act of cronyism. To everyone's surprise, Greg Larsen showed up as the lead consultant. Hosken's friends had a way of recycling through PUD contracts related to IT. During his review process, he confided in Doug that he might be returning. During his interviews with project staff, no one held back. They gave him detailed examples of how the project was being mismanaged.

In November, four programs went live, including Payroll and Human Resources. The remaining 12 programs that were late were still a work in progress. In front of the entire EBS team, Steve instructed me to meet with Elaine Gentilo, the HR manager, and inform her that the promised eApps for the employee benefits portal wouldn't be available until Phase 4 and possibly not until early 2005. I was reluctant to carry water for Steve. He was the manager, and it was his responsibility. But he made it clear that I needed to go to the human resource manager and explain why her benefit apps wouldn't be ready when we promised. At any rate, I went to see her. I didn't want to complicate an already touchy situation by telling her about my department's struggle to get a paid contractor to perform and how management had not backed up my department when we made them aware of their deficiencies. I did my best to explain that it was more complicated than any of the experts estimated. It became a pattern when there was bad news to deliver, I was sent to deliver it.

In reflection, it was apparent the EBS managers and team had big yellow streaks down their backs when it came to taking any responsibility for their actions. If the implementation contract had been properly written and overseen, at least the initial 16 programs could have been completed on time, and the ensuing struggles and controversies could have been avoided.

November brought more change. Greg Larsen was announced as the new EBS Director to replace Steve Currit. There was no open competition for the position typical for a public entity. Greg's hiring deepened the sense of distrust between the employees and management. It was, at the very least, questionable ethically to hire an independent reviewer during an engagement, but that didn't seem to bother Joe Jarvis.

In December 2003, the commissioners were again asked to extend the implementation contract deadline and agreed to pay an additional $995,900 in fees. The cost now stood at $5.6 million and Jeff Smith, the project manager, announced that the project's total cost would likely come in at $13.2 million.

One of the commissioners asked why the cost kept accelerating so far beyond the original figure. Without even hesitating, although he characterized it differently, Smith replied that they had purposely lowballed the actual price to get it approved. They knew it would cost appreciably more and had expected all along to come to them for more money.

Not one of the commissioners balked at his statement. In many organizations, purposely lowballing a bid would be considered an act of deception, even unethical. But the Hosken regime was in power, and deceit and sleight of hand and murky ethics were standard operating procedures.

Sometime in December, Jeff Smith signed off on a progress payment for the contractor, despite the long list of contracted issues still not resolved. This upset many in the department, particularly Doug.

The system was scheduled to "go-live" sometime the following year, so Mark and I had begun drafting organization charts representing what we thought the IT department should look like after the implementation was complete. The software would require personnel to develop and apply new skills to keep things running smoothly. I submitted several iterations of our new organizational concept to Steve Currit, and he kept sending us back to the drawing board. He finally relented, probably because he knew that he was leaving the project and said I could take our current model to Joe Jarvis for approval. I submitted our work to Joe at one of my weekly supervisor meetings with him and got his tacit approval to move forward implementing it.

Mark and I were pleased. We began to draft job descriptions to match the positions we had identified in the new organizational structure. The process prescribed that we would submit these to Human Resources for salary review and grading. But first they needed chain-of-command approval, which meant that the documents required signatures from the EBS Director and the Executive Manager of our business unit. You guessed it: Currit and Jarvis.

Even though Joe had approved our organizational model, he suddenly put a stop to our implementation with no real explanation. Things languished in this state for months until I finally convinced Larsen, who had assumed his new position with the district, that we needed to define our new organization to be prepared to support this new system. I suggested that I retain an external contractor to perform the work. I had consultant money in my budget that I could use to get it done. I managed to convince him to let me proceed and drafted a scope of work to publish with a request-for-proposal from prospective consultants. I found out later why it was so easy to get approval for this.

Eventually, the commissioners approved a contract with Deloitte & Touche to conduct this study. Deloitte was Hosken's old stomping ground, and he knew how to use the consultants as his lever to get what he wanted. Based on my scope of work, Deloitte would study the IT department for the most effective reorganization post-PeopleSoft implementation.

In January, Jan Frisk of Deloitte performed the study and recommended a new IT organization chart. It's not insignificant to note that Jan Frisk was a former associate of Greg Larsen. The reorganization plan that Deloitte delivered offered two options. My exact title did not appear on either one of them. I don't remember my heart sinking in surprise. Since Currit showed up in my department, it had been apparent that his job was to eliminate me. Since they couldn't find any other grounds to terminate me—so far—perhaps they had to pay a consultant to erase my position on an org chart.

I didn't feel that insecure. There were other titles that did not appear on Jan Frisk's organizational models. I had spent more time with her during her information gathering than any other district employee. She was impressed with the work Mark and I had done researching best practices for post-implementation support and the department organization options that we had developed. I even detected more than once her confusion over why we had not just run with one of the options we had already developed. Coincidentally, that month, I had reached my 55th birthday, which, combined with my 20 plus years of service, qualified me for retirement. However, my benefit would have been significantly reduced because of the difference between my age and the normal retirement age of 65. In reality, I had no intention of retiring, or walking away from this job, though the thought had crossed my mind. In short, I did not believe that Jan Frisk, or her work product, had eliminated my position. My skillset was in there somewhere. This would become a key issue when my conflict with the PUD came to a head sometime later.

The department's dissatisfaction, particularly among Doug, Mark, and Ken Smith, the senior leaders, continued to percolate. The three of them began to formulate more written proof of the failure of the implementation and the mismanagement of the entire EBS team.

The project woes were becoming more widely known. Doug decided on his own to challenge Jeff to resign in favor of someone who was more capable and experienced. He said that it was the honorable thing to do. With just the two of them in Jeff's office, Jeff stated that he was hurt and surprised at Doug's suggestion. He was, naturally, a bit defensive about the project and his performance. That was the whole encounter. Unfortunately, others apparently tried to make this simple, short, and private exchange into something that could be used against Doug. A formal harassment claim was made. To Jeff's credit, he went on record with an account of the meeting that matched what Doug gave. No disciplinary action ensued. I doubt the idea for the harassment claim came from Jeff.

Despite the open hostility toward Jeff's apparent practice of paying for uncompleted work, he continued to authorize payments. The oddest aspect of the unnecessary drama was that neither Steve nor Jeff ever confronted the contractor over their unfinished work. Why would they let so much vital work slip as they did, then try and push it off on others? I believe they were weak managers, afraid of anyone who disagreed with them. If they challenged the contractor, it would be tantamount to admitting wrong. They both exhibited an unwillingness or inability to listen and assimilate credible feedback they didn't like or that didn't jibe with their way of seeing things.

They were modeling Charlie Hosken down the color of his socks.

If management had put pressure on those being paid to perform the work instead of putting pressure on the IT staff, the outcome would have been different. What if, throughout the project, Steve and Jeff had faced issues objectively? An objective, well-adjusted manager, wouldn't react so emotionally to a subordinate's dissatisfaction. They would ask questions, try to understand their point of view. What if the contractor staff had been forced to rise to the occasion? I'm confident what happened in the next few months could have been avoided. Instead of peace and cooperation, PUD staff experienced anxiety, disillusionment, fear, self-doubt, and above all, anger. I'm convinced all this angst was according to Hosken's plans. His management style thrived on chaos, and he had set in motion forces that would harm lives and ruin careers.

In early January, Mark Bolz and Ken Smith entered my office with a sheaf of documents detailing the PeopleSoft contract deficiencies from the very beginning until the end of 2003. They wanted to take their concerns directly to top management. I reasoned with them, reiterating how important it was to use the chain of command like we had for everything else. They were disappointed with my position. After the others left, Mark lingered behind and closed the door. He chastised me for not "goring the bull." He believed that their documentation would prove that the project had been mismanaged.

We talked, and he calmed down. He pressed me on what I thought would happen to us if we didn't get some resolution to their concerns. Through all this, I forced myself to remain optimistic. Mark finally left my office. I didn't think it would do much good, but I planned on bringing up Ken and Mark's observations with Greg at our next meeting. We had been browbeaten by managers over protocols and respecting management hierarchy when raising issues. So, I was determined to push their complaints as far as I could, beginning with Greg Larson.

Little did I know this whole fiasco was about to blow up in everyone's face.

The next morning, Mark suddenly appeared in my office. He was visibly upset. The documents they brought into my office the day before somehow had found their way into a reporter's hands at the *Wenatchee World*. Mark was livid. The documents had been scrubbed of names except for Mark's. His name was all over it. The reporter wanted him to come in for an interview. He refused. But the reporter wouldn't take no for an answer. It would be better for Mark if he cooperated because they intended to publish an article with or without his help, and his name would appear prominently.

This wasn't how I wanted the problems resolved, but now the genie was out of the bottle. Things were going to become very public, very quickly. The chips would have to fall where they may.

CHAPTER 5

The Dog Whistle

On the morning of February 29, 2004, a mild wind braced the frosty lawns and rooftops across a quiet Wenatchee while the temperature barely rose above freezing. Amid the chill, the *Wenatchee World* arrived on doorsteps across the city. It wasn't long before the front-page article, just above the fold, "System Error—PUD: Missed deadlines, cost overruns, internal conflict…Is huge computer project out of control?" boiled the blood of executives and EBS managers up and down the PUD hierarchy.

In his punchy style, the reporter, Martin Salazar, laid out the same litany of charges Mark, Doug, Ken, and I had been making for the past year. There had been cost overruns in the millions, failed implementation due to mismanagement, and inexperienced EBS managers were learning on the job and failing miserably at it. Mark emphasized the main objection the IT professionals had raised from the very beginning—the PeopleSoft system they had purchased was not appropriate for the organization's size and needs.

Several times in the article, Mark Bolz stated his concerns about the new program's overall failure. The reporter didn't stop with Mark. He had spoken up and down the EBS command chain, quoting many of the key players. But Mark was the only IT employee who had gone on record with his complaints. Not coincidentally, Ken Smith's name had been removed from all the documents dropped off anonymously at the *World's* offices. This put Mark in the spotlight, as far as the *World* reporter was concerned, and he became the star witness to all the alleged problems at the PUD—as well as the chief target of an internal investigation.

Mark's decision to participate in the *World's* investigation had come about with a lot of soul searching. He, as well as many of us in the department, knew what was at stake. In the days before he agreed to speak with Salazar, he had come into my office seeking advice. He told me the reporter had been relentlessly pursuing him since the papers arrived in the *World's* offices.

We sat down to discuss the situation, Mark, Doug, and I. Mark asked us if he should refuse to cooperate. Or should he go to the man's office and tell him everything he knew of the ongoing fiasco?

I felt for Mark. He was not only a competent manager and

technologist but a highly ethical individual. If he did cooperate, every bit of his pent-up anger at managing the chaos surrounding the EBS project would get aired publicly. Mark's career at the PUD would undoubtedly come under scrutiny.

As the three of us discussed the situation, it gave us time to reflect on how we had gotten to this place—that critical problems could not be solved internally, but only through flashing a public spotlight on them. We realized that perhaps it had been the secrecy and urgency that caused us to misunderstand Hosken's real aim. As we began to itemize the pattern of events, their real intentions became clear to us. First, the department had been excluded from the brown paper exercises that the EBS team performed with all departments to document their processes. This is the first step in completing the requirements definition phase for the EBS project. We thought it was curious at the time since we were the most process-oriented department in the utility. And we were the only department that had implemented a continuous improvement framework that gave us standard and repeatable processes. Our department's omission didn't raise a red flag at the time, but it was other omissions that certainly did.

Later, the EBS team realized it had not inventoried the reports that the new system would be required to produce for each department. I was tasked with presenting a request to the commission for more funds to remedy this oversight and given a responsibility to find a contractor to produce these reports. In a face-saving effort, I was told to get the project done as soon as possible. But when the project team interviewed department personnel to catalog the necessary reports, the IT department was again excluded.

Finally, in 2004, we were informed that there were no funds in the EBS project to implement the PeopleSoft Helpdesk module, a necessary and vital function.

As we recounted all of these episodes, the implications of our situation suddenly clarified. It wouldn't be necessary to document our department's processes, to produce internal reports, or to implement a helpdesk if they planned to outsource the entire department.

According to his operating pattern, Hosken's ulterior motives and secret strategy were to outsource the entire IT department to one of the companies his buddies were now working for. To satisfy his ambitions, he had subjected the whole department to open ridicule at the hands of his favored team of displaced and underqualified staff. They had done Hosken's bidding in taking every opportunity to diminish the work ethic and professionalism of 22 well-prepared and competent individuals. Not only did this make us angry, but it also proved to us that we were all expendable.

More than likely, it was Doug's effort to unionize the department that had delayed or dissuaded him altogether of their efforts to follow through with their plans. And now that the newspaper was in on the crisis he'd created at the utility, Hosken would not be able to work in secret any longer. If there was one entity in town that had Charlie Hosken in their influential sights, it was the *Wenatchee World*. They had a history with Hosken, and the newspaper's memory was as deep as its archive. A few years back, Hosken and his wife had been charged with assaulting a neighbor, creating a public scene unbecoming the local utility manager, a scandal the *World* covered in detail. Then the *World* had sued Hosken and the PUD under the

Freedom of Information Act to access the secretive Port Ludlow retreat minutes. If the paper sniffed out a potential controversy, the editors and reporters would not hesitate wading into the fight to expose any wrongdoing to public scrutiny.

After our conversation, it became apparent we didn't have any friends at the PUD. So there was no reason for Mark to hold back. The very next day, he went downtown to speak with Salazar.

Mark sat for several interviews, pointing out the players, the decisions that were made, and the project's gross mismanagement. He mainly focused on the inexperience of the managers chosen to run the project—Steve Currit and Jeff Smith. To his credit, Salazar was able to get all of the players on the record, dialing up Steve, Jeff, and Joe to gather their comments on the record.

The article angered management at the highest levels. It detailed Mark's accusation that the EBS managers didn't have the qualifications to either source the project or direct its implementation. And that the entire project was out of proportion for the utility's employee count. No utility in Western Washington had purchased an enterprise system with more than 16 modules, while Chelan had purchased 42 modules.

The accusations of mismanaging, overspending, improper payments for work that wasn't performed, inadequate implementation of the new system, and collusion in approving contracts to preferred vendors didn't sit well with management.

Joe Jarvis was livid. Steve Currit and Jeff Smith denied everything, claiming the entire project was under control.

Roger Braden was blamed for deciding to proceed with the project. In contrast, others sang the praises of the new features that would soon be available to the employees due to the enhanced functionality—if and when the entire system was finally installed and operating.

In the article, Jarvis defended the project's expenditures, going as far as saying, "I'm pleased with what it's costing us so far." As the PUD's CFO, Jarvis knew that the project's cost was far beyond initial projections and far beyond what anyone had imagined it would cost.

The heart of Mark's observation was that "We have a management that is learning on the fly…and I don't think there has been an honest accounting of this project to our… commissioners and…executive management."

But there was more: no feasibility study had been performed to determine whether the project was worth the cost. The IT department's warnings that the project was at "a significant risk of failure" had been ignored the previous year.

Then there were the suspicious hires. In fall 2003, in response to IT and other internal employees' concerns, Jarvis had ordered a review of the project. He hired an outside consulting company to evaluate its progress. Greg Larsen, Charlie's former coworker at Deloitte & Touche and a former PUD employee and IT manager, showed up to perform the assessment. A month after his findings were accepted (they concluded the project was behind schedule and deadlines needed to be extended), he was hired as the new EBS manager to replace Currit. A sweetheart deal that frustrated many within the department, with Bolz calling it a conflict of interest to hire a consultant who had recently been under contract. Had Larsen been promised a job if he gave a favorable report?

The blowback from upper management was immediate and forceful. The internal counsel hired an outside law firm to conduct a review. While that sounded promising, the attorney who arrived to take up the investigation was Erin Rice. Mark refused to meet with her because she was an associate at a Seattle law firm owned by Eileen Lawrence. Lawrence had a longstanding personal relationship with the PUD General Counsel Carol Wardell ever since law school. As a matter of fact, Eileen Lawrence represented the PUD at the Public Employees Relations Commission hearings during the second unionization attempt by the Information Technology employees.

This put Mark in a squeeze. If he didn't show up for the interview, he jeopardized his employment. If he did cooperate, he feared the investigation was nothing more than a show, and management had already made up their minds what they intended to do. They denied Mark's request to have an attorney present. After he refused again to cooperate, he was suspended.

Everyone in the department, including myself, was shocked. According to Gil Sparks, the interim HR director and the utility's labor lawyer, Mark was suspended for insubordination.

Mark claimed his suspension was retaliation. Gil Sparks disagreed and was quoted in the *World* as saying, "I do not think…that's an accurate reflection of the situation."

At first, Mark was suspended with pay—then management upped the stakes. He was informed that his suspension would be for one week without compensation. If, after that, he refused to cooperate, he would be fired.

To protect himself Mark then filed a whistleblower petition with the PUD, asking to protect his employment under that statute. Mark's dilemma wasn't lost on the other employees. It sent a chill through every one of us. We were all expendable if we didn't bend to the will of management, even if that led us in a direction that countered our training and best judgment. I had honestly believed that my tenure and accomplishments somehow protected me. I had also assumed that honest input from professionals who had spent their lives and education studying their vocation would be prized or at least considered.

Now I had to consider where that thinking had gotten Mark. He had placed his career at the PUD in jeopardy by speaking the truth, thinking this would bring responsible people to their senses, and they would finally listen. And he was in the process of being publicly slapped down.

The message management was sending came through loud and clear to everyone. Doug continued his organizing activities, bringing in a new union representative to work with him and the staff on securing a new and positive vote to unionize. The Washington Alliance of Technology Workers filed a representation petition. The vote the previous fall had fallen short of what was necessary to unionize, but this didn't deter Doug's new efforts. As long as they were in the process they were protected. The organizer couldn't believe that the PUD was interfering so much. The public sector was usually pretty sympathetic. This was more evidence that their intent all along was to eliminate the entire department and all the personnel in it.

PUD management immediately filed a motion to block the IT department members from holding a second vote on unionization. The PUD lawyers claimed that the Public Employment Relations Commission (PERC) rules required one year between attempts to hold elections. But since the first election had not taken place under PERC authorization, the motion was denied, and the election moved forward.

During this commotion, I was called into meetings to discuss my involvement with the article. Greg Larsen and Gil Sparks, still operating as the human resource manager, grilled me on what I knew and when. Greg had the memo we had written the previous year, the one addressed to Joe Jarvis detailing the project's shortcomings that Steve Currit had refused to send up the chain of command. Greg asked me at least three times if I supported the contentions in the memo.

Three times I said yes, I did.

I also explained how I had advised the authors to respect the organization's chain of command. They had wanted to march into Jarvis's office and slap it on his desk. I talked them into letting me take it to Currit, my direct supervisor. Neither Greg nor Gil made any other comments. The meeting ended abruptly. I had no idea what they were fishing for or if they were fishing at all. The memo contained complaints voiced on several occasions by different people to managers, executives, and consultants. So, it shouldn't have been a surprise to Greg, primarily since he had performed the outside evaluation as a consultant just last fall.

While Mark's suspension continued, I made a promise to him that if he wasn't restored and made whole, I would go public with our observations about the project and file a whistleblower complaint too.

March was a challenging month for Mark and the IT department. Erin's investigation continued, focusing on improper payments to the implementation partner for work that hadn't been completed. Mark still hadn't been reinstated, and he feared for his job. He continued to feel persecuted for his efforts to shed light on the problems. In an article that month, even the *World* observed that PUD management seemed more interested in deflecting blame for the project's issues than they were to solve them.

Mark's concern that Erin Rice wouldn't be objective in her assessment pushed him to approach the county prosecutor's office. He delivered a packet of documents to the County Prosecutor Gary Riesen, showing that the contractor had been paid nearly a $500,000 for work it hadn't completed. Riesen took it under consideration. In the same week Mark turned to the county prosecutor, Jeff Smith approached the commissioners for another $700,000 to jack up the total cost of the software to over $14 million, nearly double the original cost estimate.

Involving the county's prosecutors' office was a calculated move on Mark's part. He thought it would allow him to invoke the state of Washington's whistleblower protections that were more extensive than what the Chelan PUD offered.

At the end of March, Mark was ordered to return to work or face immediate discharge. When he returned that Monday, he found he had been demoted. Most of his staff involved in the implementation were transferred to Ken Smith. In all, seven of his staff were moved out from under his supervision. His Applications Development Supervisor position now only included two staff and minimal responsibilities.

Mark again went to the newspaper, claiming the reorganization was management's way of retaliating against him.

In April, Erin Rice completed her investigation. The results were anticlimactic. Ultimately her findings didn't solve anything. Rice determined that there had been no mismanagement of funds since the contract allowed the PUD to issue credits for work that hadn't been completed. Jeff Smith claimed it was his intention all along to ask the implementation contractor for credit for work outlined in the scope of work and paid for, but never performed.

It's doubtful Jeff was telling the truth. The so-called "credits" had become a convenient way out of the situation for him. If he intended to ask for one, why hadn't he just stated that months before when he had been confronted about paying for uncompleted work? Why had it taken all this turmoil and trouble before he declared his intentions? Since Steve Currit had made it clear that I was never to see the contract, I had no idea what terms were involved. Neither did I, nor anyone else, have any idea if the credits clause actually existed or if it had been recently negotiated to absolve him of mismanaging funds. Further, even if the credits clause had existed the entire time, how was the team to address the work that was being credited? Did those tasks just go away, or was the unwritten part of the formula to assume that the IT staff would take responsibility for anything the implementation partner didn't complete?

If I had known the terms included an option allowing for credit for unfinished work, I could have headed off all this trouble by making Mark and Doug aware of Jeff's plan. Instead, his actions led many of us to a different conclusion. Jeff might have been absolved of mismanaging funds, but the investigation didn't absolve him of a tragic failure to communicate with all the parties involved in the project. His management failure cost the PUD untold hours of productive work from key employees, creating a genuine lack of trust between management and the functional staff. In a well-managed operation, staff shouldn't have to work under a cloud of fear and suspicion. Everything the EBS team did was shrouded in secrecy. That's the atmosphere the EBS team had created.

In my estimation, Jeff's behavior was pure Hosken. Whether EBS management was told directly to make life as brutal for the minions who worked under them, or whether they surmised that this was what their chief wanted, I cannot determine. Only the EBS managers know why they treated the IT team like expendable parts, failing to communicate, ridiculing their efforts, and persecuting them when they offered their professional opinions. But we do know Hosken had handpicked this team, elevated them to their positions, and given them their charge. All roads of inquiry lead to his demented way of operating that was chaotic, vindictive, secretive, and unpredictable.

≋〖≋

Subsequently, Mark was denied whistleblower status by the commissioners. There didn't seem much enthusiasm on the commission's part to challenge any of management's decisions. Nothing would stop Mark from criticizing the project. In March, it was discovered that the new payroll system that went live the previous November was miscalculating retirement contributions. This news hit the newspapers quickly and became another black mark on the project.

We continued to work on the implementation, and most of the critical modules were slated to be implemented by the coming July. The new customer billing system went live in June, and it worked very well. We had hired a different implementation partner specializing in these systems to implement the billing module, not the original contractor. Everything went smoothly when it went live, and we all breathed a sigh of relief.

Around this time, I was informed by the EBS team they had no funds in the budget to implement the helpdesk, and without that module in operation, my department would not be able to support employees' service requests. I was assigned to make a presentation before the commissioners to ask for a change to the contract allowing the software's implementation.

Early in June, I made a presentation to the commissioners, requesting authorization to implement the helpdesk software. I had no idea how tense, and potentially explosive the environment was in the boardroom that day. Two reform candidates for commission seats were in attendance, as well as multiple public critics of the manager and commission. Werner Janssen, the candidate for the seat held by Dave Pflugrath, was there. Werner had previously initiated a recall petition against Commissioner Bob Boyd, known to be a staunch Hosken ally. Although the recall effort had failed, it revealed the cozy relationship between the general manager and certain board members.

RECALLING THE BOYD RECALL ATTEMPT

Also in attendance was Ann Congdon, candidate for the position held by Jim Wall. The two reform candidates had already been vocal critics and advocates for change. Even though I had not met either one of them at that time, there must have been suspicions regarding collaboration between myself and these candidates.

After presentations such as mine, executives and commissioners usually ask questions. Hosken jumped right in, asking how many full-time-equivalents (FTE's) would be required. I had anticipated that question and had a clear answer: one part-time employee. We had already identified a local college student familiar with the program, and we wouldn't need to hire any FTEs. I was pleased with myself that the presentation had gone so smoothly. I was about to wrap up my presentation by asking for their authorization to proceed when a man in the audience asked a question. Since commission meetings are public meetings, the audience is allowed to ask questions.

I believe the man was a well-known, vocal critic of many

of the utility's recent decisions. I turned to field the question from him, and he asked if the cost for the helpdesk had been included in the original contract, "Or are you not aware of the terms of the contract?"

A potentially loaded question. The helpdesk had been overlooked, and I had my notions why. I don't believe it was an accidental oversight, but this wasn't the place or the time to discuss my suspicions. All I needed was the commissioners' authorization, and we would soon have what we needed. So, I took the out the questioner gave me.

I used his exact words to frame my answer. "I'm not aware of the terms of the contract." Much to my surprise, the answer elicited snickers from the gallery. I then turned to the commissioners, and they authorized me to move forward.

Pleased with the results of my presentation, I turned to scan the room for an available seat. The room was packed. The only one open was between the gentleman who had asked me the question and a woman who turned out to be Ann Congdon— the second reform candidate running in the fall election for commissioners.

I seated myself, and Ann, whom I'd never personally met before then, leaned over and asked me a question. I leaned toward her to answer. I didn't notice the commissioners' scrutiny or the concern that rippled across Bob Boyd's face. But after the meeting concluded, I noticed Bob Boyd, a large lumbering man with a wide girth and nearly bald pate, climb down from the dais and engage Joe Jarvis in a long conversation, casting furtive looks my way. In my naiveté, I was convinced he was complimenting me on a well-thought-out presentation. That notion would prove untrue.

I was scheduled to give another presentation the following week. In my weekly meeting with Joe Jarvis, I was told I wouldn't be making the presentation. I inquired why. He told me the commissioners had concerns about my behavior the week before.

I was stunned. They weren't troubled by the quality of my work but over a perception of my attitude toward the project. I tried to reason with Joe, but he was adamant—the commissioners thought I had a bad attitude toward the overall project. I then did something I had not planned on. I asked him if he saw the value of my employment. His response told me I was on the verge of being fired.

Jarvis essentially said my future was being discussed at the moment.

I left the meeting convinced I was on the way out of a job I loved. The reason for my dismissal, whatever they told, was evident. I had become a political liability. Individual commissioners had become convinced I didn't support their decisions, and I was somehow a threat to them.

Over the long July 4th weekend, I finally sat down and wrote my whistleblower petition. I took the opportunity to include many of the incidents when I was slighted, sidelined, and persecuted for merely speaking the truth. I knew these items alone wouldn't constitute a reason for the petition, but I wanted my side of the story on the record. I also wanted PUD legal counsel to be aware of the behavior by these managers that could, and should have, put their utility at risk. I then focused my whistleblower claims on the same issues Mark had raised—

contract collusion and government misconduct. I also stated that I feared retaliation for speaking out.

I pondered the ramifications of mailing this petition. In some ways, I had nothing to lose. I had been told directly that my career was being weighed in the balance over a seemingly innocuous situation. On the other hand, I had everything to lose. It was doubtful a similar position at my level would arise in town, and we'd be faced with leaving. My aging parents had moved to Wenatchee to be close to us, and Deanna and I had planned on helping them as we could. My kids and grandkids were local, and the thought of moving away from a lifetime of friends and family to find another job didn't appeal to me. Naturally, we agonized over this decision. It would be disruptive regardless of what we decided. In the end, we both agreed that I needed to exercise leadership on this issue. Up to that point, I had been following prescribed protocol to support the contentions of my department personnel and to try to make their professional lives better. It was time to assume a different role.

On the 4th, I set aside my work and focused on spending time with family. My only sister, Carolyn, was in town from her home in San Francisco. She usually visited my parents on the holiday weekend, and now we were all together. My older sister had been an inspiration to me her entire life. She was diagnosed with a severe thyroid condition as a child and the radiation treatment, which was then in its infancy, ended up giving her cancer. At the age of 28, she had to undergo a radical mastectomy to save her life. Her health was always tenuous, but she had a productive and seemingly healthy life for nearly three decades. She never married, but she had carved out for herself a satisfying life in San Francisco, and even though we were separated by miles, she relied upon my parents for moral support. She often traveled with them to the UK, France, Australia, Mexico, and all over the U.S.

Working as a "dresser" in the wardrobe department for the Arts Association of San Francisco, she dressed some of the most recognizable actors and actresses. She purchased a home with her partner on Potrero Hill overlooking the bay south of the Oakland Bay Bridge. Every time we visited, or she came up to Wenatchee, she seemed confident and happy, truly content with her life. In her late 50s, cancer returned, but it never turned her bitter.

That weekend, we boated on the Columbia, picnicked in the scenic hills, and explored the beautiful country along the river. She wanted to cruise the river, which we did. When we went ashore, I had to carry her, but she was off once her feet touched the dry land. She climbed to high points and basked in the glorious surroundings of the gorge.

We ate and drank and laughed together as if none of us had a care in the world. It crossed my mind, as it must have for all of us, that she was dying. But on this day, we put her health aside and simply celebrated the love and contentment of being together as a family. Living in the moment is one of the most challenging things to do when life presses in around you, threatening to swallow you. I sensed that Carolyn just wanted to be with us as if every moment was precious to her. She wasn't one to complain about her health or even mention it. The memories of that day are still sharp in my thoughts.

On the 5th, I returned to the world as it was to me then. I

decided to mail the petition to everyone concerned: The Chelan County Prosecutor, Gary Reisen, Stacy Jagla, the Chelan County PUD auditor, Charlie Hosken, all the commissioners, the Washington State Auditor, the Attorney General of Washington, and to Scott Kane, my attorney.

I returned to work with apprehension. I knew the ax would fall, but I didn't know when. It was challenging to concentrate on work, but I soldiered on. No one measured my work performance. They were only concerned about my stance on the "great project" that had become a dividing line of loyalties. You were in Hosken's camp or the doghouse.

At the end of July, I was called into a meeting with Joe Jarvis and recently hired HR director Randy Stedman. I was told my position had been eliminated, and I was being "reduced in force" as a result of the Deloitte study conducted earlier in the year. On my attorney's advice, I made them aware that I considered the action to be retaliation. They placed a severance package offer in front of me and asked me to sign. When I refused, they gave me three weeks to consider it.

The turn of events that day wasn't unexpected, but it didn't matter how much I had prepared myself mentally—I walked out of the building with a heavy heart. I had poured my heart and intellect into this job and invested so much energy in nurturing the employees—a bit of darkness crept into my thoughts as I walked through the front doors for the last time as an employee.

It took me a day or two to think about my situation to let my anger subside. I spent some time with my attorney, Scott Kane. We reviewed the proposed severance agreement, and we decided that it had been designed to insult me. They proposed paying me through the end of the year and continuing my benefits, but I had to agree not to criticize the PUD or any of its employees publicly. I had every reason to believe that Carol Wardell wouldn't hesitate to cancel my payments if she heard even the flimsiest accusation about me speaking out. Their terms were nothing more than a muzzle.

Additionally, I had to agree that I could never be rehired at the PUD in any capacity, which I found odd if my layoff had been an actual "reduction in force." Hosken had no problem moving people around to different positions once they had plateaued. But in my case, I was too much of a political risk to have around. I decided to let the severance offer expire.

I was officially separated from the PUD on August 12, 2004. Unemployment was such a rare situation for me. I had never experienced it, but I was confident that we could weather the difficulties ahead even without a severance. Receiving unemployment benefits helped.

My attorney, Scott Kane, had dealt with the PUD on many occasions, and his strategy was to have me appeal the denial of my whistleblower petition. Once that happened, he was confident he could get me reinstated. While I looked for a job in the ensuing months, I pushed appeals to the denial of my whistleblower petition higher and higher up the legal ladder—all with no success.

In early August, Carolyn came back to Wenatchee again. She stayed with my parents, and it was apparent that she was in her last days. Whenever I saw her, she kept her problems to herself. She was weak, and she wanted to spend as many days as she could with the family. I didn't get to see her much, but she made every effort to be cheerful when I did. I remember the last time I saw her. We took her to our local airport for her flight home. At the airport, she didn't wave goodbye, she waved farewell. It was an emotional scene—one I will never forget. In so many ways, she was such a brave person to face her difficulties with such grace.

Deanna and I discussed our plans for the future. She wanted to take six months off and travel to get away from all the Wenatchee drama. After some consideration, I didn't think that would be a good idea. Though we could manage six months away, I didn't want to have a large gap on my resume. So, I plunged into a serious job search.

Two weeks after my termination, Carolyn was admitted to a San Francisco hospital for the last time. She died shortly afterward. In a moment of reflection, I thought of how difficult her life was, but how she persevered and refused to give in to her illness and lived as full a life as one had. I was very proud of her, but her death struck me as another moment of loss in a season of loss.

Weeks later, my parents, wife, and I flew to San Francisco for my sister's memorial service. We took advantage of Alaska Airlines bereavement fares, which included an automatic upgrade to first-class. When we were boarded and settled in our first-class seats, coach passengers streamed past us. Greg Larsen appeared at the door, and I tried to catch his eye, but he brushed past us down the aisle. He also boarded our connecting flight to San Francisco. Later I found out that he was attending a meeting in the Bay Area at PeopleSoft, where they met to quash rumors that the company was up for sale. Mark Bolz had predicted such a scenario back at the beginning of the project.

If PeopleSoft did sell out to Oracle, the new owner wouldn't support PeopleSoft very long. The PUD would be forced to migrate to a new system.

In the meantime, the town was ramping up for a vote on new commissioners, and the two reform candidates were getting lots of attention. I met with both Ann Congdon and Werner Janssen. They wanted to have a better understanding of the morale inside the PUD. I told them everything I knew and had witnessed, blow by blow, campaigned with them, and contributed to their efforts. I had gained my freedom when I hadn't agreed to the PUD's severance agreement.

Several controversial issues were driving this election cycle, and one of them was the burgeoning expenditures and growing controversy surrounding the PeopleSoft project. When Mark was suspended and I was fired, it added a great deal of momentum to their campaigns.

WERNER VS. GOLIATH

On a Tuesday evening in October in a downtown park, I

hosted a picnic party for my staff. A time to move on. As a parting gift, I gave each of them a whistle and told them never to stop doing the right thing. It was another moment of loss for me but a joyful sendoff.

The fall was hectic. After I exhausted all my appeals for whistleblower protection, my attorney filed a $1.2 million claim against the PUD. This was a preliminary step to filing a lawsuit. Scott hoped to negotiate a settlement before ever going to trial since he believed jury trials could go either way, no matter how strong a case I had. I thought that Charlie Hosken and his cabal were getting away with running roughshod over an otherwise well-run organization, and it truly bothered me that he could just force out those who were strong voices of opposition. The legal firm of Lacy & Kane, a partnership between Steve Lacy and Scott Kane, was not a glory-seeking entity. They did not look for cases that would be controversial or widely publicized simply to enhance their presence.

They did not advertise or vocalize it, but the impression of most in the valley was that they represented the common person. If you wanted to fight city hall, they were the firm to retain. I did not know Scott well. Some of my children had been in Mrs. Kane's elementary school class as they grew up in the valley. I saw Scott occasionally at youth athletic contests and in the grocery store, but we had seldom been in each other's presence very long. The man and the company were very pragmatic and realistic. There was no "We're going to make these guys wish they never messed with you!" Every move was cautious and calculated, to the degree that they retained other attorneys to evaluate their chance of success. They employed forensic accountants to assess damages, so they had a basis for monetary claims. Every move was translated into a potential cost to the client so that taking the next step was always your decision.

When he asked me about filing the claim, the first step toward either a settlement or a lawsuit, all he did was provide me with the information he had gathered independently. Through contacts he had in the community and in the utility I had just left, he had found that nearly everyone was dumbfounded at my dismissal. Of the dozens of Chelan PUD employees he had queried, only one said my termination was justified. The community leaders he spoke to said it was beyond comprehension. So, given that, he said it was up to me to decide whether to move forward. It was my reputation, my community standing, my friends and neighbors, my coworkers, my parents, my kids. Did I just want to walk away and put it behind me, or did I feel like the injustice was enough to try to hold them accountable? I told him there wasn't any choice. Both Deanna and I felt like we could not just let them get away with it. Walking away would make it look like we had accepted that we deserved this. We needed to fight.

Since Mark had retained Lacy & Kane when he was first suspended, my first assignment was to ask him if it was okay for his attorney to represent me. We needed to be comfortable that we did not present a conflict of interest for each other. Once that was resolved, Scott offered to take my case on contingency. Essentially, they wouldn't get paid unless I prevailed by way of settlement or jury award. Scott and I made our best attempt at calculating a dollar request for the claim. His primary objective was to get me reinstated at the PUD in some capacity. He felt that the threat of legal action and the overwhelming expression of support from the community would cause them to relent and make amends so that we would incur minimal damages and would be able to stay in the Wenatchee Valley. The alternative, he believed, was that they would undoubtedly settle my claim. The utility had settled a lawsuit from a former maintenance worker the previous year. It would do the same in 2005 in a suit filed by the fired project manager for the fiber-optic implementation. However, it became apparent over time that they intended to give no quarter in my case. They would not discuss reinstatement. They would not discuss settlement. They would not make any admission of mismanagement or unfair treatment. They wanted to make an example out of me. If you haven't connected the dots yet, neither had I until that moment. It became evident to both Scott and me that Charlie Hosken, and by association those who blindly served him, wanted to destroy me. Literally. I am convinced that he would have liked nothing more than to see my marriage fail, to see me ruined financially, to see me shunned and ridiculed, to see me destitute and even suicidal.

While we were waiting for the PUD to respond to my claim, Mark and I had some invitations to convey our story to community groups. We took advantage of these since, otherwise, our situation's public perception was influenced by the utility's press releases and coverage from the local media. One of the more exciting opportunities that came our way was speaking before the North Central Citizens Coalition for Responsible Government. It was a significant moment for both of us, an opportunity to reflect on the values that inform those who govern us. We didn't have a lot of discussion about how we would structure our presentation. It just seemed that we naturally fell into our roles. Mark related the "project" story based on the document archive he had assembled over the past couple of years. Without condemnation, he made the case that the software was too big and expensive. The project team was inexperienced and uncooperative. The implementation partner was opportunistic, and no one wanted to admit that anything was amiss, dooming the project from the beginning. Mark's presentation was impressive and an eye-opener for those in attendance.

For my part, since I was the one who had been "cut loose," I wanted to be a bit more personal. I wanted the audience to know that we did not choose to be where we were. We had no hidden agendas. Everything we had done was in the interest of the utility and the public. I wanted to make sure they were aware that we were dismayed with the role we were asked to play in this project, but we were not bitter. We had a job to do, and we dedicated ourselves to performing that to the best of our ability. I conveyed the entire timeline to them, from my initial meeting with Hosken all the way up to the ill-fated commission presentation. I did not draw any conclusions about why things had transpired the way they did—instead, I left that up to them. They had good questions. Some wanted to know my education and background. Or how Charlie Hosken could have ever attained the position as general manager. And if I would have done anything differently anywhere along the way. We felt good when we left that evening. Through exposure and synergy, we got the truth circulating in the valley. We had become change agents.

In November, I received a terrific offer from the Municipal Court of Seattle to become their Director of Information Technology. It was a firm offer, but it would require a move since it was so far away. I accepted it but postponed my start date since I was still interviewing with a utility, a cooperative in Hermiston, Oregon. I felt far more comfortable moving to another utility, which would not require us to move our household, as it was only 160 miles from Wenatchee. When they made me an offer, I accepted right away and informed the Seattle Court I was no longer interested in their position.

CHAPTER 6

*Once There Was a Way
to Get Back Home*

After my termination in July 2004, the *World* broke a story that laid bare some of PUD's inner workings. To the public, managers expressed satisfaction with the computer system's changeover progress, but in private they wrung their hands among themselves. Through a public record request, the *World* received over six thousand pages of internal documents—memos, reports, emails, and attachments, along with other material. Many of them had been redacted, but reporters pieced together an altogether different story than their public announcements.

In email exchanges, managers complained about the

contractor's progress to implement the new system and the staff's inability to complete the project. While they vented to each other about the project's status, they told the commissioners another story—one much rosier. Jeff Smith gave glowing reports to the commissioners while simultaneously discussing the possibility that employees were sabotaging the project.

That theory took root from a passing remark by the contractor project manager. I know he expressed this opinion to managers when he was asked about the implementation's slow progress. He responded that the employees were sabotaging the project. To me, this excuse became a crass attempt to deflect blame away from the contractor's inability to perform. Still, it wended its way up to senior management, who embraced it as gospel. Managers glommed onto it as a plausible reason for their problems and refused to look any further. These managers did not have the expertise to solve the problems facing them, so they found a way out. Instead of listening to expert advice, they chose not to ask too many questions.

Proof that this theory had taken root surfaced that previous September during the first union organizing meeting, chaired by Joe Jarvis, to discuss employee concerns. Jarvis, without asking any questions, boldly accused the entire IT staff of sabotaging the project. He had already decided. This accusation was an outright lie, and it insulted the integrity of the professionals working on the project. But EBS management was so convinced that we were bent on ensuring their failure they undertook a cyber forensic investigation. It was possibly the most bizarre incident of the entire saga.

After the *Wenatchee World* exposé on the project, Greg Larsen came to me and told me I would need to grant network access to a contractor that the district had retained to do some investigative work. I told him I would have the network personnel take the contractor's application, determine the access he needed, and escort him through the District Security Department's registration process. Larsen told me that this person did not need to go through our standard security procedures. He indicated that this contractor and his software would have unlimited access to the company's network and software systems. I reminded him that the North American Reliability Corporation (NERC) Critical Infrastructure Protection (CIP) cybersecurity standards had become mandatory in 2003. I reminded him that we had spent a lot of time and effort, bringing ourselves into compliance with the requirements in lieu of serious penalties if the utility failed a future audit. He indicated this was an emergency and that we would suspend the requirements this time. My network folks were livid, with good reason.

Much later, In January 2017, Mr. Larsen told the commissioners and the *Wenatchee World* that the PUD had never been the object of a cyberattack—but we had. In 2002 our network was infiltrated with a "malicious bot." It was an early denial of service virus that originated in China. We noticed it began to affect the performance of some of our servers. It took us several days to eradicate it. Probably more than anything, it left us with the awareness that we were potentially vulnerable and that we needed to adhere to our protection procedures diligently. With that experience in mind, the man in charge of our department was now directing me to ignore those safeguards. This was as sinister as it was dangerous.

Management had obviously retained a "ghost" contractor to

ferret out evidence of insubordination, misconduct, or sabotage on the part of IT personnel. We gave him the requested access, and for days, he ran his software against all our active and archived email files. To the best of our knowledge, he found absolutely nothing. We had circumvented our security procedures established under a national critical infrastructure protection mandate so PUD management could find evidence to support their contention that the IT staff was responsible for their project failures. In the end, they found nothing useful to cover their posteriors.

It wasn't until much later I realized their desperation and pettiness. No one was entirely sure why they would go to the expense and the risk of this effort unless someone had led them to think they would have a payoff. It is probably purely coincidental that our own Ken Smith, who had been one of the most vocal critics of EBS project management, was recently promoted to a position that absorbed most of Mark's direct reports. And his girlfriend, a contractor implementation team member, had recently been hired into the PUD HR department.

It is true that managers created an atmosphere of fear and intimidation that bred mistrust between management and staff working on the project. This mistrust blinded them to the low morale and tense working conditions they created. The managers directly channeled Hosken's attitude toward employees he couldn't control or bend to his private purposes.

The signs of low morale existed everywhere. The attempt to unionize the IT department was a desperate move to protect their jobs from whimsical management decisions. Mark's talking to the newspaper about the chaos in the department was a slap in their face. Staff turnover on the functional team and in

IT directly resulted from mismanagement. The whistleblower complaints filed by Mark and me, though both were denied, served as temperature gauges for an entire department's demoralization.

Instead, from the first moment Currit stepped into the IT department, he, Smith, and the rest of the EBS team operated in secrecy, failed to communicate effectively, and treated everyone on my staff, including me, with suspicion and contempt.

Ultimately, it was this management incompetence that led to the events that finally unraveled the Hosken era. Beginning that summer, a slate of reform candidates campaigned to replace two long-time commissioners.

Werner Janssen and Ann Congdon openly challenged Hosken's management style, spending, and personnel decisions. They both promised in their campaign that once they sat on the commission, they would reign in Hosken. Janssen accused Hosken of creating an atmosphere of fear and intimidation, leading to the problems that had become public fodder. Congdon, likewise, said she would hold Hosken more accountable for his personnel decisions. And both the candidates stated they would look deeper into my firing, with Congdon claiming it was unnecessary.

They both believed, and rightly so, the commissioners had become too cozy with the executive management and had surrendered their oversight responsibility. That would all change when they were seated on the board.

Reading the tea leaves was one of Hosken's specialties. He sensed trouble was brewing, and he needed to protect himself and his power. In the summer of 2004, he tasked Carol

Wardell with fashioning a new governance policy that would limit the elected commissioner's authority. Her new policy, which she claimed she had drawn from the policies of various governing boards throughout the state, would effectively end the commissioners' ability to oversee anything except broad policy decisions. According to the carefully worded text, the commissioners would have no power to review any executive managers' decisions. They would also have no access to any personnel files or any personnel.

When this became public, people saw it for what it was— executive management's attempt to shield themselves from scrutiny by the very people elected to do so—it completely backfired, only fueling more opposition to Hosken and his regime. Janssen and Congdon won their primary contests in September, putting them on the November general election ballots.

In an editorial piece published in the *World*, the writers stated it was a "clumsy attempt…by the lame ducks to codify the status quo." They further noted that if the policy were to put into practice, it would "be illegal for the new commissioners to raise the issues that led directly to their election." If taken literally, it would make the commissioners nothing more than "cheerleaders."[9]

---

9 "The Role of the Cheerleaders," Editorial Board, The *Wenatchee World*, November 26, 2004, p. A09.

Both Congdon and Janssen came out sharply against the proposed new governance policy. The policy would hand Hosken, Wardell, and a few other executives' exclusive power to run the PUD. Congdon claimed that PUD executives needed more oversight and direction, not less.

Current commissioner Jim Wall disputed that notion. He pointed to all Hosken era accomplishments, listing accomplishments in fishery conservation, wind power generation, and fiber optic build-out. Even with those accomplishments in the books, Janssen and Congdon's message centered on Charlie Hosken himself and his pugilistic management style, resulting in a negatively charged atmosphere among the employees. One of the egregious clauses of the proposed policy, which bothered both candidates, was that commissioners could not criticize executive managers for their "personalities." Hosken's management style, which related directly to his personality, was one of the candidate's most significant issues. Perhaps just as sinister was the restriction that commissioners would not be allowed to review management decisions, would not have access to personnel files and could not be involved in human resources matters. So, conceivably, management could outsource and eliminate an entire department without commission oversight.

After the two reform candidates won in the general election, unseating Wall and Pflugrath, the commissioners focused more narrowly on the governance policy's ratification, scheduling a vote for late November over the Thanksgiving weekend with many citizens and the newly elected commissioners were out of town. Jim Wall was eager to see it passed before he stepped off the commission. They received so much public criticism from Werner and Congdon that the commissioners held off on the vote, tabling the controversial policy until after the newly elected commissioners were seated in January.

CHELAN COUNTY P.U.D. COMMISSIONERS

Dan McConnell, Cashmere

The first part of 2005 was busy for the new commissioners. While Bob Boyd made it known early on he didn't think he could work with the new commissioners,

Gutzwiller said he'd keep an open mind and asked Werner and Congdon to do the same.

They were both sworn in on January 4. Janssen wasted no time. In his first commissioner's meeting, he presented a proposal to revise the whistleblower policy. The current policy had become a point of contention when the PUD rejected both Mark's and my petitions. The objectivity of the executives reviewing the petitions was called into question. Management responded to that criticism, expecting that there would be a call for a change. They formed what they called an audit committee, which was tasked with reviewing all internal complaints.

The new committee was composed of Stacy Jagla, who had always been an Internal Auditor, and several executives, including Wardell and Jarvis. The *World* editorials and citizen comments openly ridiculed the makeup of the committee. People saw it for what it was, a disingenuous attempt to appear transparent. The very people who would review complaints were most likely responsible for the problems. Janssen's proposed new policy would require all internal complaints to be reviewed by an outside attorney or firm to give an objective opinion. This proposal wasn't rejected outright. Instead, commissioners tabled it to provide them with time to study the current policy. The whistleblower policy would continue to be discussed throughout the year, with the established commissioners regularly throwing up objections that postponed any decision.

At the end of January 2005, the news broke that Oracle had completed its acquisition of PeopleSoft. This news created a real measure of speculation both inside the PUD and within the community. Had Mark's prediction come true? The question remained that the new buyer could orphan the PeopleSoft product, leaving the PUD needing to undergo an expensive migration to a new system.

The controversy over the PeopleSoft program wouldn't die, particularly because Mark Bolz wouldn't let it. Shortly after Oracle announced the purchase, they began laying off 5,000 employees, mostly from their new acquisition. Mark was quoted in the *World* reiterating his comments from back in 2003 when he warned this was possible. He went on to say that management had ignored the technical experts who had recommended Oracle for this very reason. It was the same story, but it annoyed the executives even more since they had already been publicly criticized for the last year over the project. Mark's comments again stung the executives and EBS managers, and they reacted. Mark received a reprimand letter, warning him of consequences if he continued to cause the PUD public embarrassment.

Mark didn't hesitate to share the letter with his friends at the *World*.

Up to her old tricks defending questionable executive decisions even at the cost of her integrity, Carol Wardell sent out an all-employee email, claiming Mark had never filed a whistleblower petition, and he failed to cooperate with the initial investigation. Mark was angry and communicated with the commissioners they needed to investigate Wardell's "integrity and character." Shortly after that, he ended the entire saga by resigning his PUD position, walking away from an $80,000 a year position.

I felt for Mark and understood his thinking. He is one of the most conscientious people I've worked with, and he refused to compromise his integrity. His willingness to always speak his mind was one of the most refreshing aspects of his character, a fearless man whom I admire to this day.

≋⃝≋

In April, the commissioners took up the new governance policy at a retreat, and after considerable revision, they hammered out an acceptable version. Contrary to what Carol Wardell had initially drafted, they stripped the new policy clean of the offending clauses that denied commissioners the power to evaluate executives and their decisions. This authority to exercise oversight would prove crucial soon when the two reform commissioners probed more in-depth into the PUD's finances.

The overall revision belied Wardell's claim that the proposed policy had brought the PUD into compliance with state law. Had the utility been out of compliance for the previous 50 years? It hadn't, and Wardell had acted in her legal capacity to attempt to subvert the oversight function commissioners were elected to perform. All at the behest of Hosken to protect him.

CHELAN COUNTY P.U.d. MANAGER EVALUATION
By Dan McConnell, Cashmere

The PeopleSoft program continued to cause problems and raise questions about its future until Oracle announced it would continue to support the legacy systems for ten more years and produce an updated version. Eventually, it would merge the systems.

In reflection, I believe that none of the three years of turmoil surrounding the software's purchase and implementation had to take place. The root causes of all the difficulties were not what the managers imagined—because it was their imagination that drove them to their conclusions of sabotage, not the facts. First, the EBS team profoundly underestimated the time it would take to install such a complex set of programs. Second, the EBS team and their executives failed to practice proven management skills of transparent and honest communication. Third, the EBS team members went about their work in an arrogant and entitled manner, failing to include all stakeholders' input. The shortened timeline and poor communication in an atmosphere of fear and intimidation resulted in the poor morale that characterized the entire project. There were no technical challenges that impeded the implementation, only human ones, and they became the roadblocks to the project's success. Currit and Smith refused to communicate openly with me. When they were confronted with technical issues by the IT staff or myself and our recommendations for resolving them, they wrote us off as imbeciles and incompetents. Or they placated us by playing games with our concerns, which Currit did, meeting with the IT team weekly, promising to solve problems but never delivering. In eight months of weekly meetings where IT managers laid out the technical issues to Currit that needed resolving, he failed to perform. Instead of delegating decisions to proven and skilled employees trained to solve these problems, he squandered our best efforts and advice by playing games and lying to us.

There were no technical issues the department staff could not have solved if they had been given the time, the freedom, and the authority to act. Instead, Currit and Smith routinely hamstrung our efforts. And behind our backs accused us of sabotage and incompetence. This behavior can be traced back to Hosken and his attitude toward people and departments he didn't trust. We, and others like us, became part of his vendetta.

In June, Congdon and Janssen asked to review the departments' preliminary budgets before the final budget was presented to the commissioners in November. This caused an uproar, not only among their fellow commissioners but from Hosken and Wardell. They both pushed back against the request, with Hosken stating publicly that the budget should be in the hands of the "experienced utility folks," not the part-time commissioners. Bob Boyd, now the commission's chairman, told them they should be on the board for at least a year before giving any input on the budget or the process.

Congdon and Janssen disagreed and took their fight to the public. The *World* became a forum for the community's discontent. In a somewhat sarcastic opinion piece, the paper's editorial writers made the case that no one expected the elected officials to write the budget because it was far too complex. But no one should expect the commissioners to sit in silence and blissful ignorance until the hired experts hand over a budget on a take-it-or-leave-it basis. No questions and no input mean no control. The issue of "control" was at the root of the conflict. The battle over the budget went on for some months, with Congdon and Janssen refusing to give up on their responsibility to exercise oversight.

The commissioners never agreed upon a revised whistleblower policy. Employees were still required to submit whistleblower petitions first to a direct supervisor or a list of state agencies. The policy would not undergo any revision until about the time of my trial, and then it was revised twice in six months.

The maneuvers Hosken had undertaken since the two reform candidates had announced their campaign the year before had all failed. The revised governance policy, stripping commissioners of the oversight authority, had failed to pass in its original form. Management never implemented the internal audit committee. And Hosken's exclusive control of the PUD's finances continued slipping through his fingers.

With the commissioners exercising more oversight, Hosken sensed the end was near for him at the Chelan County PUD. If he didn't have total control, he didn't feel safe in his position.

My surmise is that it spoke to his personality defect, the very issue Wardell's original policy was designed to protect. He needed total control to run the organization the way he saw fit, which was difficult to accomplish in a public entity such as the public utility.

In November, Hosken announced that he was resigning as GM and taking a new position with a large water district in Southern California. It's easy to say that he had been looking at least since the previous spring to secure a position at his level. Was it his loss of control of the full commission that led to his packing off to Southern California? My sense of Charlie Hosken is that he didn't want the job unless he had total control. He was not a consensus builder. His style of management was more confrontational than conciliatory.

There was a lot of mixed feeling about his leaving. Many of the rank and file said good riddance. Some executives he worked with lauded him for his accomplishments, as did some commissioners. During his tenure, they built the fish bypasses, the re-licensing of the power generation dams was well underway, and they completed other major renovation projects. In retrospect, I believe any of the former GMs would have completed these projects as well. They were all competent engineers and administrators.

More telling is the fact that shortly after Hosken resigned, Joe Jarvis announced to the board it would be necessary to increase rates 2.5 percent per year for the next six years. The final decision on rate increases wouldn't come for another 11 months. In December 2005, the PUD adopted a budget that was 10 percent higher than the previous year. It also included positions for 40 new FTEs. This budget increase was significant because we had been under strict guidelines to reduce the workforce for the last three years before my termination. I had to submit extensive documentation to backfill vacancies, and it was even more challenging to fill newly created positions. Yet, in Hosken's last budget, he increased the workforce by six percent, and the PUD went through six years of rate increases.

One way to judge the effectiveness of any initiative or investment is to evaluate the payoff. A fundamental justification for spending nearly $17 million on a robust PeopleSoft program was that it would create new efficiencies and reduce overall staffing costs. With 40 new positions coming into the PUD in 2006, it contradicted their claims about the new efficiencies, putting the lie to the reason they had eliminated my position. This observation wasn't at all lost on my attorney, Scott Kane, who was still evaluating my chances of winning a lawsuit based on unlawful termination. I believed I'd been unfairly terminated without cause, and management needed to be held accountable for their actions. Throughout 2005, Scott continued unsuccessfully to negotiate with the PUD to close out my case. At some point, we would have to decide to move forward with a lawsuit, but Scott wanted to explore every option before we went that route.

In 2006, the commissioners started a national search for a new general manager. They had one internal candidate in Joe Jarvis. But as they proceeded through a series of interviews early in the year, they eliminated Jarvis as a candidate. The commissioners intended to bring in fresh blood, someone with a different management style who would relate better with the employees and the community.

Rich Riazzi, an experienced utility executive, came aboard in

October 2006. His 2007 budget, approved in December 2006, kept expenditure growth to 4.5 percent by deferring $27 million in operating expenses and construction projects. The PUD's finances were troubled, and he commissioned a cost of service and rate study to determine if rate increases were required. After 11 months of analysis, they approved increases to take effect on January 1, 2008. In 2009, the PUD experienced an $18 million shortfall and had to ask for volunteers to participate in an early retirement program. While various factors contributed to the PUD's continuing financial challenges, the sparse snowpack that reduced power generation was one of them, the years following the Hosken era were lean financially.

Not to be lost in this activity is the fact that in July 2006, Mark's father, Dennis Bolz, announced that he was running for the commission seat held by Gary Montague, the last existing commission member whom I believed was a Charlie Hosken sycophant. Dennis made it clear that his campaign was not about revenge for his son's mistreatment but rather his belief that there needed to be more financial oversight and accountability on the board. He did say that he believed "people in an organization have a right to criticize…to question. If you take that out, you lessen the organization."[10] But his primary focus was keeping a close eye on PUD finances and helping to build consensus. Dennis Bolz narrowly defeated Gary Montague in November 2006. Mark and I actively supported his candidacy and in February 2007, following his initial victory, we sent him a gift: a silver whistle in an oak case. On the case lid is a plaque engraved with the words: "In Case of Belligerent Management, Just Blow – Congratulations, Mark and Gordon." He has been

---

10 "Father of Former PUD Dissenter Vies for Commission," Christine Pratt, The *Wenatchee World*, July 25, 2006, p. A03.

reelected three times and is currently in the middle of his fourth term. I believe people feel he has been faithful to his campaign promises and contributed significantly to positive financial decisions at the utility.

I believe commissioners exercising their oversight capacity kept the PUD from going into a financial and management free fall. They worked with the new GM to deal effectively with the financial issues. Public oversight by capable local citizens who took their responsibility seriously to protect the public's interest in local power generation went a long way toward stabilizing the PUD's finances. A stable PUD benefited all the citizens and businesses in Eastern Washington who depended on inexpensive and reliable power every day.

≋🛆≋

To bring Charlie Hosken's story full circle, he began his employment at Imperial Irrigation District in El Centro, California, in early 2005. In June of 2007, he was terminated without cause, the press release stated. The district lost $230 million on a natural gas hedging bet that went south on his watch. Though the program had begun before he arrived, the board held him responsible for not supervising it closely.

≋🛆≋

In January 2005, I started my new position with Umatilla Electric Cooperative. Though it was a much smaller utility with no power generation, my new job presented me with some unique responsibilities that challenged my skills. Working at

Umatilla Electric over the next four years was probably the most rewarding part of my information technology career. Large utilities typically compartmentalized technology, creating groups defined to address specific needs with boundaries that limited creativity and collaboration. My jobs had always been limited to business information technology, managing the business systems that supported back-office and front-office business functions. Hydro operations, power trading, system control and data acquisition (SCADA), metering technology, telecommunications, and electronics also had their specific duties and boundaries.

My peers' common lament in Northwest public utilities was that it seemed fine for anyone to breach business technology boundaries by creating single-purpose databases, acquiring and installing software, and producing their proprietary reports. Still, all the other technology functions at the utility were "secret squirrel" stuff that one would never dare to encroach upon. I don't think I can assess the volume of missed opportunities for collaboration.

At small electric co-ops, technology permeates every part of the operation and is integrated and managed under one umbrella. From the time I first came through the door at Umatilla, I was given responsibility for things that I could not even touch for the previous 23 years. Besides the usual business systems, networking, and computer support responsibilities, we developed an outage management system integrated with the geographical database, enabling outage monitoring in real time.

We implemented an automated warehouse inventory control. We handled security, including the building alarm systems, perimeter intrusion detection, and cameras. We were responsible for the telephone system. We acquired and implemented a computerized vehicle locator system and enhanced it with automated job order capability, enabling us to dispatch approved orders directly to handheld devices in the field.

The last thing I managed before leaving Umatilla Electric was the automated metering infrastructure. We installed a system that enabled meter reading and meter management over our electrical distribution wires. The system required new equipment at all the utility's substations to enable the latest technology. We then replaced all the commercial and residential meters in our service area with meters with remote metering capability. It was fascinating and gratifying.

I was fortunate to become part of an organization that allowed me to feel good about my professional capabilities again. It was validation that I was right and that my departure from Chelan PUD had nothing to do with my capabilities.

I had moved on with my life, but I still bore the marks of those years under Hosken's boots. The PUD denied my claim for damages, but Scott, my attorney, continued to negotiate, hoping they would settle. He was cautious about going to trial, telling me on more than one occasion that it was risky, and the financial rewards often weren't worth the effort. The PUD had a history of settling lawsuits resulting from terminations. They terminated Ron Yenney in 2004, and after he sued over his departure, they settled with him. My attorney was hoping they would do the same with my claim, but his efforts proved fruitless by the end of 2005.

We had a frank discussion about what I wanted to do. My

attorney, Scott Kane, consulted with a law firm on the coast specializing in calculating what I might win in terms of back pay and damages in a lawsuit. The results of their research on similar cases, at face value, didn't seem worth the cost of time and resources to move forward with a lawsuit. After talking it over with Deanna, we both decided we wanted to sue. My anger had crystallized into a determination for vindication. I wanted a public airing of the issues surrounding my termination. Even with Charlie Hosken out of the picture, I believed it was vital to hold the executives who created the hostile workplace accountable. The only power I possessed would be a lawsuit.

Scott Kane was cautious in advising me to file. Though the deadline was drawing near, he persisted in researching the likely outcomes. No one entered a lawsuit without the belief that they could win, and the PUD's unwillingness to settle had some ramifications in his thinking. They knew my termination was a highly charged affair, but they refused to make it go away. Scott weighed these elements, and after considerable research, he believed we had a chance of winning. It wouldn't be easy, and the verdict could go against me, but we decided to move forward.

Before the statute of limitations expired, we filed in Washington State Superior Court in June 2006. It would take another three years to get it on the docket. But we used that time to prepare.

With Deanna and I living in Hermiston, about 160 miles south of Wenatchee, neither of us saw our aging parents as often as we did when we lived closer. Deanna's parents lived in Quincy, just south of Wenatchee, and my parents were in a senior living home in town. On one of our weekend visits to the area, we stopped by to say hi to my folks before we left town and found my father sitting on the sofa in a confused state. He'd suffered a stroke, so we rushed him to the hospital. We stayed an extra three days to make sure he had the care he needed. After a few days in the hospital, he was on his feet and seemed on the road to recovery. Both of us realized that it wasn't best for us to be so far from our parents. In 2008, I took a new position at Grant County PUD, which moved us closer to Wenatchee, where the trial would take place. The move served a couple of purposes. We were closer to our aging parents, and my employment in Washington returned me to the state retirement system, where I could complete my years for full retirement benefits. And my attorney's office was only 40 miles up the road. I would spend more time there, taking part in depositions and meeting with Scott. Ultimately the trial took place in early 2009. It had been a long wait to get into the courtroom, and I would be glad when it was over, but there was still a long road to go before my ordeal was over.

Just when things were looking extremely positive for the future, my mother took a nasty fall and struck her head. She lapsed into a coma from which she never awoke. She passed away on September 11, 2008, just days before we began depositions for my trial. Early the following year, we moved my father to a retirement home in Ephrata, very near my new employment.

CHAPTER 7

Like Atticus Finch

With the death of my mother, it was hard to return to preparations for the upcoming trial. It seemed that at crucial stages of my troubles with the PUD's management, beginning with that first meeting with Charlie Hosken back in 1998, my life was marked by a family hardship. I don't say tragedy because life and death are so much a part of our existence, but the passing of my family members, first my sister and then my mother, only amplified the personal anguish as a result of my travails at work and my ultimate termination.

After investing 23 years of growth and relationships in one company and a group of people, my termination left me with a determination to one day have my case heard before an impartial audience. The sense of wrong in how I was treated had marked me in incalculable ways that the grief at my mother's passing amplified. I was smart enough to know that a trial is not therapy in any sense of the word. Still, I also knew that there are very few aspects of our lives that we control and that we need to do everything we can, whenever we can, to prevent others from stealing any of that control.

It wasn't a foregone conclusion that I would have my day in court before an impartial jury. Though I never hesitated in my resolve, my attorney was more cautious. He was hesitant to take a case to trial, citing the uncertainty of trials by jury. For the previous two years, he had attempted unsuccessfully to negotiate a settlement with the PUD representatives. He lamented their refusal to negotiate in good faith. They were intransigent in their determination to vindicate their decision to terminate me. He concluded that any form of a settlement would be an admission of guilt on their part.

One of the keys to convincing Scott that the trial would be successful was the attitude of the PUD's executives he encountered during his many conversations. He also saw me as a straight shooter and a well-respected employee, whose story would garner a jury's sympathetic response. All the factors combined, he plunged ahead with preparations for the trial.

The depositions began in September, and by the time they were concluded, Scott had even more reasons to believe we would prevail. The depositions had further convinced him the PUD's witnesses wouldn't come across well on the stand.

The maneuvering between the two lawyers, Scott and Lew Card for the defense, started early. During the depositions,

Scott told Lew Card that he didn't want anyone on the defense witness list in the courtroom until it was their turn to testify. It surprised me that this point was open to negotiation. Who would sit at the defense table representing the PUD wasn't settled until the trial began and the judge ruled.

The trial began on February 17, 2009, nearly five years after my termination. The first several days were taken up with preliminaries—jury selection and rulings on motions. It was decided that Erik Wahlquist, staff attorney for the PUD, and Randy Stedman, PUD HR Director, would assist Lew Card. Scott wanted Carol Wardell prohibited from sitting at the defense table, which she tried to do the first day of trial since she was on their witness list. The PUD had a plethora of well-dressed attorneys in $1,000 suits right behind the defense table comprised of folks like Wardell, former manager Roger Braden, and Stedman. On our side, it was just Scott, his paralegal, Laurie Anderson, and myself. It felt a bit intimidating.

After the jury was selected, the judge ruled on the motions in limine presented by Scott and the defense. Lew Card submitted a long list of motions for the judge to rule on that sharply focused the trial.

Essentially the defense's 33 motions narrowed the trial down to one central point. The trial would not examine the process or the justification for selecting the PeopleSoft software. The PUD decision to acquire that particular enterprise system wouldn't be discussed or examined, neither would my job performance be used as a reason for my termination. Both sides' motions narrowed the complicated case down to one question: was I was laid off because my position was eliminated—as the PUD contended—or was I terminated in retaliation for my filing a whistleblower petition? As a consequence of allowing the trial to be focused on that one issue, Scott agreed to set aside the "constructive discharge" argument. By abandoning that argument, none of the imaginary performance issues that Steve Currit created by overloading me with work when he first came into the department would be entered as evidence.

Finally, it was time to begin, and each side took a turn with opening statements. It was interesting to note the differences in style and content of both attorneys. Lew Card was a short, unremarkable balding man hidden under an expensive suit. He outlined a logical argument, essentially claiming that I was unqualified to work on the PeopleSoft program since I was primarily a "hardware" expert. Since I had no practical experience with the new system, I wasn't the proper candidate for management positions once the IT department was reorganized. He claimed to have emails from my associates claiming I wasn't qualified to oversee the completed project. He intended to prove these allegations in the course of the trial.

I could tell that Card's remarks were powerful—but I knew his evidence would not prove his arguments. We had witnesses who could refute their contentions that I had not participated in the project and could refute the contention that the Deloitte study recommended eliminating my position. Most importantly, we knew Card had utterly misunderstood one of his primary pieces of evidence—Doug's email about my ability to participate in a particular technical capacity on one of our projects.

Scott's opening took a different slant altogether. At six foot five with dark hair and dressed in a sport coat and tie, Scott had a commanding presence, but not one he used to intimidate. He possessed a calm and respectful demeanor, particularly toward the female witnesses. This behavior would be noticeable when he questioned Stacy Jagla and Carol Wardell.

Where Card focused on the purported logical process behind my termination—as they told it—Scott zeroed in on the impression my termination would make on the jury—a 23-year employee tossed aside because he dared to speak up. Scott always maintained that we needed to impress upon the jury the emotional and financial consequences of management's decision to terminate my employment. Scott anticipated their sterile, technical approach to presenting their argument, and he expressed confidence our version of the story would sway the jury.

The trial began on Wednesday, February 18. After more work on the motions, the jury was seated, and Scott opened up the session by calling our first witness—Greg Larsen. Scott's strategy for calling Greg as a witness for the plaintiff was to ask him, "What was he doing there in the first place?" He wanted the jury to hear from Greg how he came to have the new EBS position. He had left the PUD three years earlier and then suddenly returned to occupy a position that was never advertised for open competition. He also wanted to hear why Greg thought anyone would feel that he had better and more recent PeopleSoft qualifications than someone who had just participated in a three-year implementation of the product.

Under cross-examination by Lew Card, Greg testified that he didn't believe I was qualified to oversee the software's operation. And as a result of the Deloitte study that laid out the new organization chart for the post-PeopleSoft installation, I wasn't qualified to step into any new management position.

By the time Greg stepped off the witness stand, Scott had effectively helped the jurors make several critical connections in my story. In the late fall of 2003, with the project in disarray, Steve Currit was reassigned to a position more in keeping with his real estate background--managing the PUD's parks.

Immediately Greg was brought back to replace Currit without any announcement or an open invitation for internal candidates to apply. They then proceeded to create a perception of displeasure with me and spread that narrative across the company.

Then they fired me. All of this went according to their plan.

After the first day of testimony, two different versions of the story behind my termination were out in the open. What the jury decided would come down to who had the most believable story. While Larsen's testimony wasn't accurate in any way, it did not upset me. I felt like he revealed on his own that he was a puppet. I knew that if it came down to comparing qualifications and experience, I would stack up very well against him.

On Thursday, Dr. Vincent Jolivet, a forensic accountant, testified to my economic loss. In the afternoon, Scott called my two expert witnesses. First, Brian Pyle, who worked with me in the IT department, and second, Mark Bolz. The defense had tried to exclude these two from the expert witness list, but the judge denied their motion. In his role as Lead Database Administrator, Brian testified that I was the expert in the department on both hardware and software for the entire PUD's business technology function and knew how all the pieces fit together. He verified that I had the background and training to understand all PUD's business technology details and processes.

I don't know if he expected a different answer, but Lew Card kept asking Brian who he went to if he had an issue to resolve or needed a decision to be made, and his response was always the same: Gordon.

When Mark testified, Scott expertly led him through his qualifications as an IT professional, his assignment to the EBS project, and his decision to leave the project. He explained how I stepped in and led the technical evaluation of the hardware required for the PeopleSoft implementation, something that the EBS team had entirely overlooked. Scott was methodical in questioning Mark about my overall expertise and reiterated several times that I "owned the network," technical jargon that meant I was responsible for every aspect of the hardware and software operation behind the business functions of the PUD. Mark was extremely effective because he had firsthand knowledge of the issues we brought to the EBS team's attention. These items would have killed their project if they had not been addressed. Mark's testimony revealed that the existing IT leadership and professionals (primarily Mark, Doug, and myself) had saved the project on several occasions. He also substantiated our chain of communications regarding project risks and potential abuses. Scott had effectively rebutted all of Greg Larsen's testimony from the previous day to the point that I wondered how the defense could continue this charade of trying to label me as obsolete and unqualified. But Lew Card wasn't deterred, and he plunged on with his strategy.

In cross-examining Mark over two days, Card worked hard to diminish Mark's credibility. Card observed that Mark had incorrectly filed a whistleblower petition and that he had refused to cooperate in the investigation. He questioned Mark on why he was not at the PUD any longer, which revealed that Mark had started his own private company in town that had subsequently failed. He tried to make it look like Mark's resignation from the EBS project team was petty because he couldn't run things.

Overall, Card's attempt to paint the picture that I hadn't participated in implementing the PeopleSoft programs failed. Mark clarified the timeline of when I took his spot on the implementation team. Card spent a lot of time on the May 2003 memo outlining the IT staff's concerns about the contracted implementation. Card's attempt to get Mark to admit that I didn't participate in the memo's drafting failed miserably.

Mark was very detailed in his testimony about how Steve Currit refused to elevate the IT team's concerns to upper management. Instead, he had us use an issues log, something that was standard procedure in the department and not a sign of Currit's proactive thinking, as Card was trying to portray it. Currit's refusal to elevate the IT team's concerns early on doomed the project's success.

After Mark completed his testimony, I believed the case was on solid ground in my favor. Card and his team had a long way to go to try and prove his case, but he was far from finished.

On Friday, the second day, Lew must have realized that badgering Mark was damaging his case, so he adopted another tactic. He decided to try to establish some rapport with the former Marine lieutenant tank commander. He drew a picture of a tank on the flip chart and talked about different roles for maintaining and operating a tank. His objective was to show that the tank could be successfully operated without someone performing in what would have been the role analogous to mine at the PUD. That's when they got into the discussion of fueling the tank, and eventually, Mark told Mr. Card that he would have blown up his vehicle if he followed the procedure he described. This allowed Mark to emphasize the importance of leadership and guidance (my role) to provide the proper training to avoid this kind of catastrophe. So, in essence, Lew's argument blew up in his face.

I felt terrific after Mark's testimony. He had been sincere, direct, and professional, and he had substantiated everything that Scott wanted to emphasize in our case, as well as eliciting laughs when he turned Lew Card's tank analogy upside down.

Next, Scott called Randy Stedman. Since he was in the room with Jarvis when I was informed of my suspension and had the least tenure with the PUD, Scott thought he might not have been as subject to coercion as some other employees. Essentially, he hoped Randy would be more forthcoming. Stedman was also on the defense witness list and would be called later when the defense presented their case—Scott would get another shot at him. Scott had what we thought was a "silver bullet" to use with Stedman but would not reveal it here. He concentrated on finding out if Randy would repeat the same talking points as Larsen so that the jury would begin to get the impression that their story was coordinated and rehearsed.

Scott further questioned Randy regarding the composition of my severance agreement, asking him why they had included the condition that the PUD could never rehire me. Steadman responded that "there was some unpleasantness with my departure." But since the severance agreement was drafted well before the meeting where I was informed of my "departure" from the PUD, Scott and I both assumed that meant some bias was involved in their decision. In other words, my termination wasn't based on the consultant's recommendation to eliminate my position. This argument would play a role later on during the defense's presentation of the case.

When it was Doug Stewart's turn to testify, he continued to affirm my credentials and qualifications. He confirmed everything Mark and Brian had testified to—substantiating my leadership capacity and abilities, affirming my participation in the PeopleSoft project, and portraying me as the PUD technology leader. But, the real impact of his testimony came under Card's cross-examination. The email between Mark and Doug, the one Card had alluded to in his opening statement that he considered a damning proof to his assertions, completely disintegrated.

Card had the email enlarged on a slide so the entire courtroom could read it. In the email, Mark asked Doug's opinion whether he thought I had the experience and knowledge to help him with a fiber optic project. Doug replied that he knew I didn't have experience and knowledge to help with that particular project, but I could help him find resources to complete it. Card thought he had found the "smoking gun" by stripping the email of its context. He badgered Doug to admit that he was referring to the EBS project. Doug wouldn't give in. Later he told me, "The presentation of the email seemed right out of a Perry Mason episode." Card thought he had cornered Doug into proving the defense's case. Doug was having none of it. He pushed back hard, telling Card he was mistaken—the email concerned Mark's request for help on the Fiber-Optic Provisioning project. It was not an admission that I could not support the PeopleSoft project, as the defense attempted to construe it. Card refused to believe Doug's answer and instead kept demanding Doug read the email's words and not interpret them.

Doug refused to give in, finally defeating Card's attempts to reframe the out-of-context conversation. Card became so frustrated that he threw his pen across the lawyer's table, hitting the judge's dais. That ended Doug's time on the witness stand.

It was true theater.

With the weekend off, I asked my family to speak forthrightly about the impact of my termination. We had every reason to believe that our case was going well. Scott had put the events into context that the defense attempted to isolate and use as smoking guns. The newspaper coverage to this point was mixed or neutral and generally fair from my perspective. Deanna was apprehensive and upset by the entire proceedings, which probably explains why she unloaded on Carol Wardell after the trial was over.

On Monday, it was time for my family members and myself to begin our testimony. Scott's strategy in calling us all to testify—my 89-year-old father, Cecil, my son, David, my wife, Deanna, and myself—allowed the jurors to gauge the emotional impact of my termination on my aged father, children, and my marriage. He also wanted to allow Lew Card to make a strategic error by cross-examining any of my family members. To his credit, Card didn't take the bait.

My father spoke about how he and my mother had moved to Wenatchee several years before my firing to be closer to my family in their declining years. He indicated it was very disappointing when I had to leave the area to find employment and that I wasn't able to move back before my mother passed away. When he left the stand, he walked by our table and patted me on the shoulder.

My son's testimony was particularly poignant. David used the analogy of a boat. With Deanna and me living nearby to my mother and father, children, and grandkids, we were all together in the same boat. If a child or a grandchild fell out of the boat, I was nearby to help and get situations turned around. With Deanna and I uprooted and living over 150 miles away, our family members were at a greater risk of not getting the help they needed from the extended family. It was a touching moment for me, and when David left the stand and walked by the plaintiff's table, I stood and hugged him, thanking him. "No," he said, "Thank *you*, Dad."

Deanna described how she'd sometimes wake up at night and find me on the computer looking for jobs and how the strain of job loss at times overwhelmed me. She said, "I'd never seen my husband break down, but one night it was like, he just curled up in my lap, and I held him like a child," she said. "Because it had just been too much."

I believe that the full day of testimony had a significant emotional effect on the jury. They understood the full scope of what it cost me to uproot myself and move to another city. It was a moving day for all of us, but a satisfying one. The players at the PUD who had orchestrated my termination knew first-hand the toll they had inflicted on my family.

I was the last witness before Scott rested our case. Altogether, I spent almost eight hours on the stand over two separate days.

Scott did another thorough job of walking me through my qualifications, my education, and my work history of increasing responsibility in information technology from my college days to the time of my termination at the PUD. After he completed that part of my testimony, I felt confident I had convincingly countered Greg Larsen's testimony.

Lew Card's cross-examination was bizarre, and again, consistent with the tactic he had tried to use on Doug Stewart, trying to trap him by focusing on certain words or phrases in memos and emails that purportedly proved the defense's case. He attempted to box me in with the same tactic. It was one that I believed was weak, but he put a lot of energy into it.

Focusing on the whistleblower petition and the phrase, "misuse of government funds," he pointed out that I had never used that phrase before the time I used it in the petition, suggesting I hadn't informed upper management of any misdeeds until I feared for my job. Then he took up the argument around the Deloitte study, badgering me to admit that I knew it recommended the elimination of my position. It was a long argument. I wasn't confident it proved much of anything, except he reiterated the facts that I had discussions with Greg Larsen on several occasions on possible positions recommended by the Deloitte study, particularly the Center of Excellence Director. My testimony spilled over into Tuesday just before lunch.

After lunch, Lew Card called his first defense witness, Stacy Jagla, Internal Auditor for Chelan County PUD. The Internal Auditor served as an independent source—someone you could present a whistleblower petition to after it was initially rejected.

I had always had a great deal of respect for Stacy, so I chose to submit my initial appeal to her. To her credit, she was the only person in the entire petition process, both in my initial submission and during all the appeals, who took the initiative to call and discuss the issues I raised in my petition. In the end, I believe she came to the wrong conclusion. She repeated several falsehoods that could have only come from Joe Jarvis or Greg Larsen. Specifically, that I had not approached Greg to discuss other positions within the PUD, and that I had declined the one offer he did make me.

Stacy was convincing on the stand that she had conducted a thorough review of my allegations. She wasn't "one of the boys" in the sense that she came across as an independent and objective person, not part of the cabal that had orchestrated my termination. But, as Scott brought out brilliantly later, the structure of the internal review process itself was biased toward the PUD. Once a petition was passed up the chain of command, the review precluded any possibility of an objective appeal. Ultimately, the appeal process was controlled by the two individuals who had rejected it in the first place—a revelation that epitomized forces that worked behind the scenes to push me out of the PUD. I often wondered at the fortitude and courage it would take to render an opinion contrary to the staff legal counsel and general manager.

After Stacy, it was Wayne Wright's turn to take the stand. Wayne was an executive director, the same as Joe Jarvis. He was also a member of the EBS Project Steering Committee during the PeopleSoft implementation. We had sent several memos up to Wayne after getting nowhere with Steve Currit and Joe Jarvis. George Velasquez, a PUD project manager, brought in to perform an audit of the project, substantiated our contentions in the memo. Wayne had not been pleased with our methods of forcing the memo to his office, but he admitted it was our memo that caused the PUD to retain an outside auditor to review the project finally. To our great disappointment, the auditor they hired was R.W. Beck, and the principal consultant was none other than Greg Larsen, our former director and then CFO, before he left for other opportunities.

The audit was nothing more than a face-saving way to admit problems existed, then to put new management in place. On several occasions, Greg dropped hints that he would return to the PUD and the IT department.

In general, Wayne defended the project and even implied that he supported the contention the IT staff had created needless turmoil and may have sabotaged the project to some degree.

Under cross-examination, Wayne admitted that he had never seen the addendum to the Deloitte study and wasn't aware the Catalog of Current and Proposed Competencies existed.

Next up was Jeff Smith, the EBS Project Manager. Lew Card concentrated on questions surrounding the negotiations for credits from the contractor for work they were paid for but never performed. Contract Amendment 7, approved by the commission in June 2004, documented that the PUD had gotten a $14,000 credit.

On cross-examination, Scott made sure to point out that Amendment 7 also added $300,000 to the implementation contract. He drilled Jeff on whether he kept the IT staff in the loop regarding the negotiations with the contractor and addressed the concerns the IT staff had raised. Jeff admitted he didn't see the need to keep us informed. Scott finished with a damning observation. Jeff had testified that they used their low-balling strategy to keep the overall costs down, yet it had allowed them to balloon the budget from $6 million to $16 million. Scott finished with Jeff, and he stepped down.

Steve Currit was next to the stand. He was an unknown as far as we were concerned. He didn't have anything to do with my termination and had been a scapegoat when all the problems arose with the project. I had seen him do some amazing things during our association, including portraying himself as having descended from "a long line of assassins" during the introductory roundtable at a customer service training session facilitated by a contracted trainer. He had continually portrayed himself as some type of martial arts expert, something that always struck me as compensating behavior. He also commented that "he could cry spontaneously" if so desired during a management planning meeting for an upcoming presentation to IT staff members who were trying to unionize. Lastly, he had a habit of yelling, "Hah, I bet you didn't see that coming!" during negotiations if he felt like he had gained an advantage. Bizarre habits that made it apparent that he was either directed to act a certain way or that he just wasn't an ethical manager. However, by the time he was reassigned, he and I were commiserating to a degree since it was apparent that he would be the sacrificial lamb for EBS project mismanagement. Lew Card used him to reassert that the project was well-managed, which Steve affirmed.

On cross, Scott went easy on Steve, only asking if he and I got along, if I observed protocol and the reporting hierarchy, and if my reviews were positive. Steve confirmed these things.

When he left the stand, Scott leaned over and said, "He didn't hurt you."

Next up was Joe Jarvis. He made it clear, as he had in his deposition, he wasn't pleased with having to be there. His attitude worked against him, in my estimation. Lew Card fed him softball questions that allowed him to vent his vitriol about the IT department's sabotage and their rationale for managing the budget the way they had. Card showed him the May 19 memo, and he said he'd never seen it. He professed no knowledge of my support for Mark's claims and whistleblower petition. He did not know of our work with George Velasquez and subsequent memo to Wayne Wright about the project. He said I never spoke to him directly about project concerns. He also had no recollection of approving a post-implementation org chart Mark and I had developed. Lastly, he claimed the decision to terminate me was made a month before they executed it and that he couldn't think of a reason to contradict the Deloitte study.

On cross-examination, Scott made Joe look foolish. After putting up the Catalog of Current Proposed Competencies on a screen and walking Joe through the recommended position's competencies, it was apparent that I fit most of the categories. It was evident to the entire court that the Deloitte study hadn't eliminated my position but had proposed I play a significant role in the department. Scott then questioned Joe if he knew of the post-implementation staffing requirement of full-time employees in the IT department. Jarvis said he didn't know. Scott asked if he would be surprised to learn that the FTE's assigned to PeopleSoft module support had doubled in the four years since it went live.

Jarvis was visibly seething by the time Scott finished with him. He was excused, and he stomped out of the courtroom.

Carol Wardell was the next scheduled witness. Card asked about the whistleblower process and why my petition was denied. He asked her if she participated in the decision to eliminate my position and draft a severance agreement. She discussed the actions of putting me on leave and my subsequent termination.

Scott's cross was much more rigorous. He initially focused on what we might call the "six degrees of separation." He led her through a series of questions to connect the dots. He got her to admit that she used to work with Roger Braden and came to the PUD from private practice at his suggestion. She admitted she was aware that Charlie Hosken and Greg Larsen were once colleagues at Deloitte & Touche. He then asked her if she was aware that Bob Fuller also once worked with both men. She was not aware of that. He further proceeded to ask her about her connection to the owner of the law firm where Erin Rice worked. She agreed the owner was a personal friend.

After he established these interconnected relationships, he went on to ask her about the whistleblower process. She agreed the petitions were designed to protect workers who were reporting government waste. She agreed she had denied both Mark's and my petition because they weren't filed in "good faith."

He then asked her where in the policy or petition is a definition of "good faith." She admitted there wasn't one. Scott noted that government waste didn't need to be reported in writing. Even if made orally, it constituted a report. He went on to ask her a series of questions about her involvement in investigating the complaints. She never talked to Mark or me personally about our petitions or earlier complaints. She did admit she advised Stacy Jagla and the commissioners regarding my appeal of the denial of the whistleblower petition. Scott then asked a penetrating question she didn't answer: "How could any employee prevail if every decision in the process is made by one individual who denied the petition in the first place?"

Finally, he asked her if she could point to the Deloitte study place where it said to eliminate the IT Director's position. She couldn't, but she said that my "box wasn't on the chart," which was in line with what Larsen, Jarvis, and others had maintained.

By the time she stepped off the stand, she appeared rattled despite the calm, professional demeanor that she typically exuded.

Lew Card didn't have any additional witnesses, which allowed Scott to call the last witness. He called Randy Steadman to the stand again. Scott had a strategy in mind. He wanted to leave the jury with a fresh impression of management's true intentions. Once again on the stand, Scott quizzed Randy, asking him if he agreed with Carol Wardell and the others that the decision to terminate me resulted from the Deloitte study's conclusions.

After establishing Randy's story, he asked him about an entry in his daily calendar dated December 2003, a full six months before they terminated me. The calendar entry was for a scheduled off-site meeting titled, "What to do with Gordon?" The invitees were Greg Larson, Carol Wardell, Joe Jarvis, and Randy. That it took place in a meeting room at the local convention center made it more sinister. Scott asked what was discussed about my position a full two months before the Deloitte study was published.

I could see the stress on Randy's face. What else could he say? The discussion was about my termination from the PUD.

It was one of those mic drop moments. It was clear to everyone in the courtroom that Jarvis, Larsen, Wardell, and Stedman had met to devise a way to terminate me, well before the *Wenatchee World* analysis of the project, well before the Deloitte study and long before my helpdesk presentation to the Commissioners. This bombshell contradicted all of their previous testimony and completely destroyed the defense excuse for my termination.

Lew Card didn't even redirect.

After eight exhausting days, I was glad for the trial to end. I had never observed a jury trial up close as it unfolded before me. After so many years of waiting for an opportunity to see justice done, I felt satisfied. The work to get to this point had been worth it. All that remained was for the two attorneys to say their final words, and then the fate of my case would be in the hands of a jury of my peers just as the founding fathers had envisioned centuries ago. Sitting ringside to this great show, I watched the closing arguments as if they were a living theater.

First up was Scott. He had prepared a lengthy presentation, one that relied as much on passion as he did on logic and evidence. If the great philosopher himself, who had defined the principles of rhetoric, had witnessed this oration, he would have smiled appreciably. He used the rhetorical tools Aristotle had defined as essential to a strong argument—logos, ethos, and pathos—logic, ethics, and emotion. His presentation left no stone unturned in reviewing first the evidence, nearly exhibit by exhibit. It was a logical, purposeful review that proved I was not only qualified to oversee the PeopleSoft program post-implementation, but I was instrumental in keeping it on track.

He also spoke of my character—witnesses had described me as honorable, trustworthy, and principled. But what impressed me most was his emotional appeal to the jury. He stirred the imagination of the courtroom, encouraging them to visualize the treatment I had received and empathizing with their fears that they may not give me the justice I deserve. From the first line of his statement, he played on their sense of justice by recasting the PUD acronym to mean Power of Unrighteous Dominion. The PUD executives possessed all the power, and they used it unrighteously to attempt to destroy my career and reputation. It was a masterful performance, and I mean that in the best sense of the word performance. His passion was convincing because he spoke the truth, and Scott didn't mince words that the PUDs defense was riddled with inconsistencies that were easy to see, and their use of power was evident. His summation reminded me of Gregory Peck's portrayal of Atticus Finch in the movie adaptation of *To Kill a Mockingbird*. When he finished his presentation, he was wrung out emotionally. We all were at that point, and the only step left before the case went to deliberation was to hear from the defense, who got the last shot at the jury.

In contrast, Lew Card's presentation was subdued, intellectual, and focused on the same mincing of words that had characterized his entire strategy. I hadn't submitted my whistleblower petition in "good faith." Card had strategically maneuvered the judge to agree not to allow me to define "good faith" on the witness stand. According to Washington State law, that definition was simply that a petition must be submitted honestly. Which I had done, so I didn't fear the jurors would misunderstand my intention. Scott had established that complaints of government misdeeds didn't need to be in writing. Card then focused on my qualifications, lack of participation in the project, and the Deloitte study, which seemed ludicrous. None of the decision-makers in my termination had even read it.

After he was finished, Judge Allan gave the jury further instructions and suggestions on how to organize their deliberations, then adjourned the court shortly after 2:30 p.m.

We had no idea how long the deliberations would take, but Scott told us to relax and wait. It could be soon or take us into next week.

I was at my father's place helping him pack for an upcoming move when at around 6:00 p.m. I received a call the jury had arrived at a verdict. My entire family and Scott, as well as Brian Pyle, one of my primary witnesses, and his wife Niki, assembled by the courthouse's rear door since it was after hours, and we paraded together through the judge's chambers into the courtroom. Judge Allan was pleasant as we passed through, remarking, "The whole clan's here." The moment made me smile. Yes, the entire clan had come to support me in this critical moment. Would I get the justice I believed I deserved, or would it be denied me? Scott was circumspect. He'd seen quick decisions go against him. And after lengthy deliberations, he'd had victories. It was best to stay steady and be prepared for the worst.

As I waited for the defense team to assemble, followed by several spectators, I reflected on the events of the week. I had no reason to think I'd lose. Scott had been masterful in developing the case, and any reasonable person wouldn't have a difficult time seeing through the PUD's flimsy arguments. But anything could happen in a jury trial. Scott had been preparing me for that outcome since the first day I began talking to him about a lawsuit almost five years before.

Finally, the moment everyone in the room was waiting for. The jury filed into the room and took their seats. I could see the relief in most of their expressions that this ordeal was over. It had consumed a week of their time, and for some, it probably had exacted an emotional toll. The judge received the verdict form from the jury foreman. Expressionless, she read it to herself first.

Then she read the verdict form out loud.

"In answer to question one: Did the defendant, Chelan County PUD, wrongfully discharge Gordon Graham, in violation of public policy?"

"Answer: Yes."

"In answer to question two: Did the defendant, Chelan County PUD, terminate the employment of the plaintiff, Gordon Graham, in violation of promises of specific treatment in specific circumstances?"

"Answer: Yes."

"In answer to question three: What are the past lost earnings, and past and future lost fringe benefits, suffered by the plaintiff Gordon Graham caused by the defendant Chelan County PUD's conduct?"

"Answer: The (significant dollar amount) adhered to the recommendations of our forensic accounting witness."

"In answer to question four: What are the general damages suffered by the plaintiff Gordon Graham caused by the defendant Chelan County PUD's conduct?"

"Answer: The (significant dollar amount) adhered to the recommendations of our forensic accounting witness."

A clean sweep. I was ecstatic. I turned to my family sitting behind me and hugged each one over the rail. I shook Scott's hand and thanked him and his paralegal effusively. They had performed wonderfully, bringing a well-organized and well-thought-out argument to the trial.

Though we'd won a major battle, the war still wasn't over.

CHAPTER 8

The Imposter Philosopher

After the verdict, I immediately experienced a profound sense of vindication. But over at the defense table across from me, the attorneys were in obvious distress and confusion. Lew Card's spirited but illogical defense strategy had been defeated, and the shock and disbelief were all over his face. A crestfallen Lew Card went into a brief huddle with a dour-faced Carol Wardell. Then, with an incredulous tone, he asked the judge to poll the jury. Lew Card was looking for a lever, a way to redeem the situation, and found what he was looking for in juror Jason Hetterle.

The only explanation Card and the defense team, particularly Carol Wardell, had for the jury verdict going in my favor was that there had to have been some mistake, some error in judgment somewhere, maybe even misconduct by a juror. During the jury's polling, it was revealed that Hetterle had voted yes on questions one through three, that I had been terminated in violation of public policy and promises of specific treatment, and that I deserved damages for lost wages, but no on question four regarding general damages. He had vacillated in his decision—he voted that I had been unfairly terminated but was against awarding me damages. A man in the middle, as far as Card was concerned. This juror turned out to be the lever Card needed to try and pry apart the jury verdict. For the PUD executives who had pushed my case to trial, there was more than a cash outlay at stake.

The company had invested considerable time and resources to fight my lawsuit, one they could have settled for a fraction of what I had just been awarded. So, it seemed to all of us who were close to the case, there had to be more than my back pay and damages motivating them to pursue trying the case. I believe they were out for vindication. Card would be quoted in the newspaper referring to the verdict as "hogwash," revealing the defense opinion that there should have been no way a jury could have reached that decision. They wanted to prove they had been right in their decisions related to the PeopleSoft project, not just correct in the way they fired me.

GORDON GRAHAM vs CHELAN COUNTY P.U.D.

Though the defense had questioned my qualifications to oversee the PeopleSoft project, the more significant underlying issue was their questioning of my character. What mystified me then, and still does to this day, was the tone-deaf arguments Card used to justify the PUD's decision to terminate me. They believed that by impugning my character, they could convince a jury I had not acted in good faith, which meant I had not acted honestly. If they could prove I had not been honest when I filed my whistleblower petition, it would automatically mean they had been sincere in their reasons for my termination. To boil the trial down to its essentials—it was my character versus their management ethic, which was, in essence, the management ethic Charlie Hosken had practiced and bequeathed to his executive team.

As hard as Lew Card worked to exclude the PeopleSoft issues from the trial, they seeped in during nearly every witness's testimony. The jury saw right through the prevarications by certain witnesses who testified that I wasn't qualified to oversee the PeopleSoft programs. In post-trial interviews, some jurors pointed out they believed several witnessed had lied. This had played out just as Scott had predicted after researching the case and deposing the PUD's witnesses. He had discerned that the way they talked about me wouldn't come across well to a jury, and he was correct.

The PUD's entire management ethic under Hosken was on trial, and the jury had found it wanting. The verdict had hit at the hard shell of "fortress PUD" as one writer in the *World* had called it. They had to find a way to justify their actions in unnecessarily prolonging my case. Then there was Lew Card and the prestige of his firm. No doubt, he wanted to redeem his firm's reputation, which I believe had been tarnished by the resounding loss.

The trial also had resurfaced old wounds that had played out before an entire community because of the PUD's management style. So, it's not unreasonable to say that this trial was more about vindicating executive management's chain of decisions and not just the sole decision to fire me. By default, the trial had become not only concerned with my termination but the reputation of executive management under the Charlie Hosken reign of terror. The editorial board at the *World* said as much shortly after the verdict when they wrote: "The verdict was no surprise because Graham's contentions fit perfectly with the atmosphere that appearance and deed suggest was prevalent at the PUD at the time, under that management... The mood was often vindictive, protective, secretive, and petty."[11] The writer described how PUD management had treated them (the

11 "Now It's Different at Chelan PUD," Editorial Board, The *Wenatchee World*, February 28, 2009, p. 10B.

press) with total disdain when asked for information about decisions that had previously been public. The Charlie Hosken regime had left public and private scars, and the Wardell legal team acted as if none of this had taken place. As if none of this mattered to anyone. As if their behavior and the lies that justified their behavior could be swept under the rug.

The defense team knew they had to deal with a soured community reputation, so Lew Card did his absolute best to make sure, using extensive pretrial motions in limine, to exclude all PUD behavior prior to this trial from evidence. In affirming the defense's motions, the judge's instructions to the jury were clear—they could not consider the PUD's past conduct in making their decision. They were to consider only the facts of the case as they had been presented during the trial.

Card sought a way to undo the verdict and searching for soft spots in the jury system was his strongest tactic. Card claimed that one juror came forward, Jason Hetterle, an IT professional with a local healthcare provider, and admitted there had been misconduct in the jury room. How he found his way to Lew Card's office is anyone's guess. Whether he came to Card out of his own volition or Card had called him, we'll never know. But by the time we left the courtroom on the day of the verdict, the defense team had identified the weak link in the jury box. Hetterle was their man.

Hetterle poured out his heart to a willing ear in Lew Card, admitting he was angry with the deliberation process. He claimed one juror, who possessed a doctorate in psychology, had unduly influenced the decision and that a second juror had made prejudicial statements about the PUD's past behavior.

Lew Card had found his lever to undo the work of the competent jury. More than likely, the PUD managers couldn't justify the cost of appealing the judgment to the commissioners and the GM, Richard Riazzi. But if they could get the verdict thrown out due to misconduct that would be a different matter. Their argument that justice had not been served went down better than asking for funds to file an appeal. If Card could get a new trial, he intended to change the venue under the assumption the PUD couldn't get a fair trial in Chelan County.

In justifying pursuing a new trial to the commissioners, Carol Wardell pointed out that the jury had been compromised. They felt that their case was strong, and if the commissioners authorized more funds to file for a new trial, the PUD could find an unbiased jury in another county. Wardell and the executive managers weren't giving up on vindicating their decisions. They instead were finding new ways to twist their story. Even independent thinker Anne Congdon was quoted in the papers agreeing to fund more litigation under the assumption the PUD "deserved its day in court." Mark's father, commissioner Dennis Bolz, recused himself from the vote since his son was one of my primary witnesses.

Researching the case further, turning over every available stone looking for a way to save his case, Lew Card found a journal entry in Scott's calendar dated July 2, 2004, where I had scheduled an appointment with him. This became Card's smoking gun argument that he claimed in his affidavit proved I had contacted him for representation before filing the whistle blower petition. Card was convinced I must have feared for my job, and that is why I chose to speak to an attorney. Scott ably parried this argument in his filings, answering the petition for a new trial before the court. He simply reiterated that several of my staff members and I had been raising issues of misuse of funds since May of 2003, and as a result, I feared retaliation. Contacting him before filing my petition was a logical step that completely adhered to my fear of reprisal.

In March, Lew Card filed a petition with Judge Allen for a new trial. Accompanying that petition was Hetterle's affidavit detailing the misconduct by individual jurors. Judge Allen put off deciding until the middle of April.

I didn't look forward to sitting through another trial. Putting my wife and family through the emotional wringer a second time wasn't something I wanted to do. None of us had any idea what Judge Allen would rule. Would she grant a new trial? Had the jury been compromised during the deliberations? None of us had any notion of whether what Hetterle was claiming was true until the local media began interviewing jurors. KOHO radio in Chelan, Washington, interviewed jury foreman Mikel Poulsen. The interview's audio was subpoenaed by Scott and transcribed for the court. Mr. Poulsen made it clear that he was confused by Jason Hetterle's comments. Poulsen confirmed there was no undue influence by any juror during deliberations and that he had a completely different recollection about comments made by other jurors that Hetterle contended were upsetting. Mr. Poulsen also pointed out the obvious question. Why did Jason Hetterle vote to support my complaint on three of the four questions if he was so concerned about the process in the jury room? Also, the *Wenatchee World* interviewed juror Brenda Berry. Mr. Hetterle had stated that Ms. Berry referred to "a history of employee mistreatment at the PUD" during deliberations. Brenda said that she never said anything during deliberations that implied the PUD had a history of mistreating employees. She stated, "I just concentrated on the facts, alone, and that was that."

≋⌇≋

While we waited for a court decision, the community forums lit up, particularly in the *Wenatchee World*. Most of the comments were in our favor, questioning why the PUD would continue to throw good money after bad. They had lost a fair trial. Why didn't they move on? Then there was one dissenter from the majority who was well informed and signed his name using a nom de plume, one that was familiar to me: Aristotle.

His remarks made me curious. He seemed to have inside knowledge of the case and knew why the defense had filed for a new trial. Then his use of the word "spitballing" clued me in that he was most likely from the defense team. And his choice of pseudonyms, the famous philosopher, intrigued my friends and me. I had been using Aristotle's ethics as a framework for my own ethical choices for some time, and to see Aristotle's name used as a cover for subterfuge was disturbing. I believe the great philosopher would have winced at his name attached to such an illogical argument.

The Wenatchee Aristotle undertook the futile task of answering the letters to the editor skeptical of the PUD's intentions in challenging the verdict. Letters to the editor were pouring into the *World's* offices. The anonymous writer continued the defense's fight to get across his central argument that Gordon Graham was lying. This ad hominem attack on my character was at the heart of their defense. They had to impugn my character to justify their position, something I believe they could never do. Aristotle insisted that I had not filed the whistle blower petition in "good faith." The writer further stated that the verdict against the PUD had resulted from juror misconduct. This seemed to him the only rationale for the jury verdict. And he also clarified that the defense wasn't appealing the decision but seeking an entirely new trial, which would only further bolster the sense of righteousness on behalf of their position. The writer lamented several times that the PUD couldn't get a fair trial in Wenatchee. He ticked off every talking point Lew Card and Carol Wardell were using to convince both the commissioners and Judge Allen to let them continue the fight.

The back and forth between Aristotle and readers of the *World* was on the surface very entertaining, but it was also very revealing. Aristotle had to be someone close to the defense or the defense attorney himself because of the details and unique language he used. Some terms that Lew Card used repeatedly in court appeared in several of the writer's newspaper comments. I feel safe assuming it was someone on the defense team or the lead defense attorney himself because of the writer's grasp of the arguments, the tunnel vision Card used to try to convince the jury I didn't act in good faith. This position had failed once, so now the defense strategy was to impugn the integrity of the jury itself, casting doubt on the fairness of the entire proceedings.

The only people vested in this argument were the defense team. I assume, and this is my own opinion, that Lew Card and his firm were under intense pressure from Wardell to rescue their case, to attempt to pull victory out of the jaws of defeat.

As entertaining as the letters were, Aristotle took his role seriously even though readers wildly mocked him. Despite our curiosity, Doug, Mark, Brian, and I decided it would be better if we didn't know who was behind the letters. Aristotle's ethics had served as a reliable guide to moral leadership, and the Aristotle of the *World* was so much like the management I'd worked for under Hosken—totally without any moral compass.

In early April, Judge Allen was prepared to rule on the accusation of misconduct. All the interested parties assembled in the courtroom, and we prepared ourselves to hear her decision. We didn't know what to expect—as Scott had said many times, a trial can go in unexpected directions. I was nervous sitting at the plaintiff's table with Scott and his paralegal, against the formidable team the defense had assembled. In a way, it was laughable that so many resources had been amassed to fight against one solitary employee. It convinced me once again certain PUD managers were personally invested in vindicating their decisions, not only in terminating me but in the claims of my whistleblower petition. While legally the trial was only about the fact that I filed a petition and whether it was in good faith, the petition's contents were not on trial. But I believe Wardell and company sought vindication for their decisions leading up to the botched implementation. Ruining my reputation as qualified to perform the job I was already doing, and impugning my character was the driving force behind all of this effort. As I sat in the courtroom thinking through the last years of chaos working under Charlie Hosken, I prayed Judge Allen would see through the sham of their accusations and put an end to this.

Judge Allen went through all the points of the defense motion, dwelling on Mr. Stride, a psychologist, and the accusation that he had an outsized influence on his fellow jurors regarding his ability to decide which of the defense witnesses were lying. Then she surprised me, and everyone, by dismissing those charges, citing comments from other jurors who had come forth about their decision. The second claim was that Ms. Berry had openly stated that the PUD had mistreated its employees for years, and it was widely known. Ms. Berry had been quoted in the *World* as denying she said anything of the sort. She had followed the rules and considered only the evidence before her. The judge discussed those claims and then summarily dismissed them.

Her conclusion startled all of us. None of the claimed behaviors, if they had occurred, had risen to the level of misconduct, so a new trial was denied.

Again, I felt that jubilation and sense of relief. But the court proceedings weren't finished. The judge, Scott, and Mr. Card had a long conversation about attorney's fees. Scott submitted his request for fees, and Judge Allen took it under advisement.

Deanna and I left the courtroom with light steps. Our long odyssey was nearing an end. We lingered in the hall, waiting for Scott to join us. As Deanna and I waited for him by the elevator, the defense team rounded the corner and stood with us at the elevator.

Carol Wardell stood a few feet from us. She surprised both of us by speaking to me. She said, "You know, Gordon, it was never personal."

Too stunned to think of anything appropriate to say, Deanna spoke up as I was considering several inappropriate things.

"Charlie Hosken made it personal," she said, a discernable tremble in her voice.

Wardell tightened her mouth and turned from us. Just then, the elevator dinged, and the door opened. She and her hired hands stepped in, and the door closed.

That was the last I saw her, but as it turned out, she still had her hand in the case, trying to the end to get her way.

An ebullient Scott and his partner Mr. Lacy joined us a few minutes later. His partner had come along to observe, and he asked me if I was pleased with Scott's work. I told him I didn't think I could have had better representation.

In discussing the day's outcome with Scott, it was still up in the air what the PUD intended to do. Would they finally accept the verdict, or would they appeal? I couldn't believe they would throw more funds at defending a case with so little evidence. But stranger things would happen.

The next day, I read in the *World* that Wardell said the PUD was considering an appeal. This set my stomach churning again.

When would this end? At this point, the money would be nice, but the vindication was even sweeter. Scott had a strategy he hoped would bring the suit to an end. He negotiated his fee with Lew Card contingent on the PUD agreeing not to appeal. Later that month, the *World* reported that the commissioners and the GM had voted not to appeal. They wanted to put the case behind them and hopefully bury the last dram of bitterness from the Hosken era. Not even counting what they had spent on defense counsel, they had just paid our side over $500,000 in awards and legal fees. It's safe to say that the entire PeopleSoft fiasco, and all the turmoil it created, easily cost the rate payers in Chelan County $20 million. From the day I innocently sat down with Charlie Hosken for a beer in 1998 to discuss my vision for the IT department to the day in April 2009, 11 years had passed. Not all of them had been miserable. I have fond memories of successful projects, enduring friendships with colleagues, and wonderful working relationships with fellow PUD employees. These achievements made for a satisfying and productive career. But all the good had been overshadowed by the struggle with Charlie Hosken and those he gathered around him. It wasn't about competence and expertise but control and power. His whisper war against a department that was wrongly perceived as inefficient and archaic had cost me and others dearly. Careers that would have flourished were interrupted and had to be restarted. Promotions that were earned were never granted. Cost-effective innovation driven by the department needs was never realized. Instead, a pet project that could have transformed the PUD's business management became a point of anger and contention. Seasons of anxiety and self-doubt ensued over issues that could have been quickly resolved by open and honest communication. The combined productive years lost to the PUD, and the value to its customers over idiotic bickering and self-serving decision-making is tragic.

I believe the Hosken era is in the rearview mirror of our community. The general managers since Hosken's resignation have brought a new culture of open communication and responsible, ethical management. For that, I'm pleased.

Epilogue:

Where Are They Now?

I wrote this in conjunction with John DeSimone as a cautionary tale. I thought it was important for the Wenatchee Valley residents and the current employees and leaders of Chelan County Public Utility District to know the details so they can recognize the same characteristics should they emerge again. I also thought it would be of interest to anyone, anywhere who may have noticed the same type of dynamic emerging in an organization they are involved with. People are fallible and, because of that, they can also be corrupt. And corrupt people who are in power are dangerous.

Writing this has been a catharsis of sorts. This story has been churning in the back of my mind since the end of my trial in 2009, and writing it down allows me to "lay it to rest," so to speak. I've never entirely subscribed to the philosophy that you need to "move on" or "put things behind you," or even "achieve closure." I did not want to die without having taken the opportunity to provide the background and details of these events to everyone who may have only seen this play out in the media.

I didn't write this with the intent to harm any of the individuals mentioned in this story. With the possible exception of a few uncomfortable questions from family members or neighbors, or perhaps a sideways glance in a grocery store, no one should suffer any consequences from me having revealed what they did. And if these uncomfortable moments do occur, they should remember that they had a choice.

The whole sequence of events was initiated by my attempt to help Charlie Hosken succeed. I was, and still am, a student of management. I recognized that our organization was getting increasingly dysfunctional in that there was no strategic vision of how technology could be implemented company-wide. This is not so preposterous when you consider that I was older than him. I had much more utility experience. I was better and more recently educated on management subjects, and I had been in that particular organization almost three times as long.

At the time, Mr. Hosken decided to initiate his oppressive management tactics against my department, we had an internal customer service approval rating of almost 90 percent. We were managing our work transparently through the company's maintenance management work order system. We were refining our approach to everything we undertook to achieve process maturity, and we included internal customers as partners to facilitate communication. And we had instruments in place to measure our performance for continuous improvement. I wanted to talk to Charlie about things like the disciplines in Peter Senge's road map to a Learning Organization. I wanted to explain personal mastery, shared visioning, and team learning to him. I also wanted to show him how the PUD's current practices were destined to damage him and the organization.

≋◊≋

Since the events surrounding the trial of 2009, most of the antagonists have either retired or relocated. Charlie Hosken left Chelan County PUD in the fall of 2005 to work for Imperial Irrigation District in Southern California. He was terminated from that position within his first 18 months due to a gas futures purchase that "went south." Since that time, to the best of my knowledge, he has been the COO for a solar energy firm named SunPeak Solar located in Southern California. The Wenatchee utility has seen three new managers since Hosken left PUD and recently advertised for a fourth, filled with a well-respected internal candidate that I knew personally.

Carol Wardell, the sometimes-controversial head internal legal counsel for the utility, retired from Chelan County PUD in June of 2015. Steve Currit retired in November of 2015. Jeff Smith retired in June of 2018. Greg Larsen transitioned from information technology into a risk management role sometime in 2020, and then retired. Lew Card continued to work for the Davis Arneil Law Firm for some time, eventually being designated "Of Counsel." This designation often identifies a semi-retired partner, an attorney who occasionally uses the office for a few clients, or one who only consults on a particular case or his or her specialty. At some point, Lew left to establish his own law practice in East Wenatchee, which is still active today.

PUD FIBER MANAGERS FIRED

Perhaps the most interesting story is that of Joe Jarvis. Joe was terminated by then-general manager John Janney in February of 2011 over a purported "inability to provide solid cost estimates on build-out of the PUD's $105.5 million fiber-optic networks."[12] His fiber-optic project manager John Smith was also terminated at the same time. One irony of this story is that Joe reached out to my former legal representatives at Lacy & Kane to represent him in a wrongful termination claim. In the meantime, after the decision in my favor two years earlier, Chelan County PUD had parted ways with the Wenatchee law firm that employed Lew Card. Instead, they retained a Seattle law firm to represent them against Joe Jarvis and John Smith. Over the next 18 months, the utility would pay over $1.3 million

12 "PUD Fiber Managers Fired Over Squishy Cost," Christine Pratt, The Wenatchee World, February 8, 2011.

in legal expenses to this Seattle firm, and the case had not even been scheduled for trial yet. Perhaps more than anything else, this fact motivated the utility to settle with the two plaintiffs in the fall of 2012. Steve Lacy, Scott Kane's partner, negotiated a very attractive settlement for both clients. The last tidbit surrounding this story is that the utility eventually asked for a list of billing rates and charges from Lacy & Kane to use for comparison in an attempt to recover some of the expenses they had paid to this Seattle law firm that had been representing it during this process. Truth is sometimes stranger than fiction. Joe relocated to Oregon and was the general manager of an electric cooperative Northwest of Eugene for over nine years. I believe he recently retired.

As for the "good guys." My attorney, Scott Kane, continued to represent clients in employment and personal injury cases with his law partner at Lacy & Kane until very recently. Scott is semi-retired from legal practice and spends most of his time riding horses herding cattle on Badger Mountain above East Wenatchee. He is also one of the Washington State Bar Association approved Tutors for Admission to Practice under Rule 6 of the Law Clerk Program, an alternative to attending law school for individuals who want to qualify to sit for the bar exam.

You have already heard about my success. Suffice it to say that Mark, Doug, and Brian have all had very gratifying careers after "escaping."

The commission reform candidate Anne Congdon is still on the Chelan County PUD board of commissioners, re-elected to her third six-year term in 2016. Werner Janssen, the other 2004 reform candidate, served one four-year term as a commissioner, was defeated in his reelection attempt, and went back to private life in the upper Wenatchee Valley. Mark's father, Dennis Bolz, is still a commissioner and was reelected to his fourth four-year term in 2018.

In Retrospect

Final Thoughts

I am aware that after hearing a story like this, it is natural to wonder what the principal players would or should have done differently. I have asked myself that question many times. Until very recently, I hadn't asked my friends and colleagues who lived through the same events, if they had it to do over again, would they have done anything differently. I even recently asked them if they wished that I had done something different.

Doug was very honest, candid, and introspective in his response. He humbled me by saying that he wished he had sought me out more as a mentor and counselor during those times. In reflecting, he admitted that his Project Management Institute training emphasized relationship building and communication in order to be successful as an individual, team and organization. He felt like he had reacted too much to the environment and forgot those principals too often. Personally, I think he is being too hard on himself. It is nearly impossible to build a shared vision with someone who is solely committed to exercising their own agenda.

Mark also observed that there really wasn't much we could have done differently. Despite efficient operations and the leanest cost that he had seen to date (and since) the IT department was, in his words, okay to kick and expendable. Charlie needed the "large IT systems feather in his bonnet" in order to build his resume for bigger things. Since there was no strong business case for a large ERP system, he had to hand it to his minions.

In his own words, "Later now in my career, if I saw the same situation, what would I do? I would try and redirect it to a much better place. I would seek to convince Charlie and the board to establish a regional ERP organization with a bigger ROI for him, which is most important to Charlie and the District. I suspect that would have failed, but in doing so, it could have been possible for him and his lackeys to learn from others and chart a better course for Chelan PUD. Bluntly, I suspect this also would have failed due to hubris and personalities."

Mark would not have known at the time, since we were being individually persecuted and my department was so fragmented, but the last major attempt I made to salvage the investment the utility had made in this software was exactly what he has said he would promote if he had to do it over again. I was working with a representative from Energy Northwest (formerly the Washington Public Power Supply System—WPPSS) and my counterpart from the IT department at Grant County Public Utility District, David Yell. Our concept was a centralized technology services organization that would have provided access to the power of the ERP systems possessed by the larger group members to all participating utilities. Sort of a public technology services company. We got to the point where we had drafted an RFP for a feasibility study. Charlie Hosken and Joe Jarvis, as well as all of our commissioners, had refused to express any support for this effort. As a matter of fact, every time I was on the agenda for the PUD manager's group, Charlie made sure he was absent. We needed financing for the feasibility study, so we asked for contributions from interested utilities. Most were looking for evidence of support from the two largest entities, Chelan and Grant. Dave could not get support from his manager without me first getting Charlie's commitment. I met with Joe and Charlie and explained the situation, and asked for dollars to perform the feasibility. They both said if the "publics" weren't willing to step up there didn't appear to be any reason to pursue it further. They actually called everyone else "public"— like we were not! Shades of the Port Ludlow retreat. Finally, Energy Northwest considered taking on the whole thing but somehow that also got scuttled.

As for me, naturally I would have liked to have seen things resolve much differently. Obviously, I have had a lot of time to reflect on these events and they have consistently been in my thoughts to one degree or another. With that said, I can honestly state that there is really nothing I would have done differently or additionally professionally during that time. From a personal perspective, I might have tried to keep my parents closer to me during the four or five years of turmoil that ensued after my termination. But outside of that, I am convinced that I couldn't have done anything more to mitigate the tragic decline of that organization during that time.

I was committed to raising the visibility and strategic importance of the Information Technology function at our utility. I had started promoting this philosophy to the management hierarchy long before my after-hours meeting with Charlie Hosken. My various supervisors at the Executive Director level had all heard my pitch that IT had become the fourth major resource available to executives to shape and operate an organization. Companies had managed the three other major resources for decades: people, money, and machines. But IT had emerged as being responsible for more than 50 percent of the capital goods dollars spent in the United States. Understanding the importance of the fourth resource and building it into the theory of business—as well as into the strategies and plans—was more important than ever before. So, the message was that executive management needed to realize that they needed to take personal involvement in making IT strategy decisions. And "executive management" meant the CEO.

I showed them my draft strategic plan, the road map on how to achieve this integration of information technology directly into the operation of the utility, and how to manage the function according to the strategic objectives of the company. I showed them the management structure that would get the whole organization involved in aligning the utilization of IT resources with the overall objectives of the utility. I explained the benefits of having a method where everyone participates so that no one questions how IT dollars are being spent.

I can't recall ever perceiving one flicker of recognition in any of them. Still, I persevered, but now I was to the point where I needed to make them aware of the consequences if we failed to make this transition. I began speaking to them about the signs of dysfunction in the organization and how they could snowball if they were not addressed. The reaction to this specific observation was a prime example of the dysfunction. The answer that I usually received was the "battle cry" of this type of culture: "take charge" and "don't let so-and-so push you around."

The existing culture was also fixated on events, rewarding quick fixes and "fire dampening." The most visible characteristic of that was their emphasis on "crisis heroism," finding someone who wanted to be recognized for accomplishment and giving them responsibility to fix some isolated problem. The company was becoming addicted to creating crises at the expense of making fundamental long-term improvements.

I kept talking to them about the realities, such as the cyclical nature of the crisis culture: the easy way out usually leads back in. Pushing harder and harder on familiar solutions only results in the fundamental problems continuing to persist.

So, this is where I was when I had my "beer immunity" meeting with then COO Charlie Hosken. I essentially revisited everything I described above (and more) assuming that he had been advised of some of it already through the management pipeline. I tried to be as positive and non-judgmental as I could while attempting to emphasize the "what's in it for all of us" perspective.

Honestly, in retrospect, I'm pretty sure what he heard was: "You suck."

To his credit, however, regardless of whether he was prepared to admit it, he heard me. He definitely got involved in technology once he became General Manager/CEO, although I think it is obvious that his motivation was less than positive. His pet project was primarily to find a way to punish me and an attempt to convince the organization that information technology personnel are nothing special—that anyone can manage IT. He did commission an IT strategy, but that was really a red herring and an excuse to justify his takeover of the IT function. We have already talked about how the only part of this exercise that was ever implemented at the company was the mismanaged PeopleSoft project, so it wasn't really a strategy at all.

You can see that we were doomed to experience these events regardless of what we did. It wasn't us. It was him, and he was in charge. During what you might call "the troubles," several of us tried to make multiple people in positions of power aware of the risks created by the manager's tactics. None of them responded positively. It wasn't us. It was them. As I mentioned earlier, I had seen some of my peers in the industry suffer through similar situations. Despite that, I can't advise anyone on how to respond. I can say, however, that my activities were in the best interests of my staff and the entire organization and because of that I wouldn't change a thing.

In 2020, almost 20 years after I first proposed the idea to Charlie Hosken, the Chelan County Public Utility District created and filled an executive-level Chief Technology Officer position. It took that long, but technology is finally integrated in the strategic planning and decision-making process.

≋⫙≋

I want to end this story with something I wrote in 2009, shortly after our trial. I think it is also a perfect bookend to complete this story.

"At some point in your life, you realize that integrity may present an impediment to acquiring some of the things you had always thought you wanted. You become aware that you will need to make some hard decisions regarding ethics and the example you want to set. You probably won't even feel it at the time, but it is possibly the most distinctive fork in the road that you will come to during your existence. In each of the two possible choices, there are practically no elements of the other. But, when the consequences begin to accrue from the path that you have chosen to take, you will find yourself looking back to identify the time when you came to that point. You will realize that the paths were clearly marked and that you gave each avenue due consideration.

"Lastly, you will realize that where you are now is the result of a conscious decision you made then. You chose this. At that point, you will need to decide if you are comfortable with who you are and the path you took at that fork in the road. I contend that if you shunned casuist ethics and situational integrity and instead turned toward honesty, regardless of the bulk of the cross that you may have to bear, that you will be comfortable with 'you.' You may, instead, realize that you took the other fork. You may or may not be satisfied with the results or with 'you' as a person. You may have followed someone else down that path with the expectation of some material reward, and the experience may have left you feeling very hollow.

"If this is you, I will testify that you can return to that signpost and consider who you want to be. It is never too late."

Acknowledgments

It is nearly impossible to adequately express gratitude for the encouragement, participation, and support I received before, during, and after writing this memoir. Immediately after the events began, countless individuals implored me to record them. Over the ensuing years, many individuals I shared bits of this story with continued to encourage me to write this story. My unequivocal thanks go to every one of them.

Right here, it would be an unforgivable oversight (believe me!) if I did not recognize the support and participation of my wife and life-partner, Deanna. I honestly don't know how she persevered and maintained through those years. We survived this together, and our gratitude and devotion to each other is, of course, private. She is prepared to be more public again to a degree because of telling this story. She is confident it will be more positive than last time.

Writing this after so much time would have been impossible if not for my attorney Scott Kane's diligence. His office had retained most of the written and printed documents from my case. This material filled seven file boxes, and he provided me with all of them. Equally as valuable were the electronic records that his office had retained, including some actual transcripts from the trial proceedings. However, perhaps the most valuable resource for the legal material in this book was Scott himself. He made himself available both by phone and email to discuss our respective memories of different events, and to fill in the blanks where things were missing. Reminiscing with him was terrific. The anecdotes and details he reminded me of were priceless. We also laughed a lot!

The other repository of information that we used was the *Wenatchee World* newspaper archives. They continually involved themselves in the events related to this story, and their records were an invaluable resource for the production of this book.

Bill Dearing provided valuable insight into the general manager's character and executive management operations at the time. Bill answered every question that I had for him and elaborated on most of them so that I could understand the nuances of things that I had not been exposed to during my career. He was a tremendous resource.

My friend and colleague Doug Stewart might have been the most willing participant. Here is where I need to apologize to Doug (and probably many other former employees) for not including all of the stories that would have supported the events we revealed in this book. As much as we were compelled to include many more jaw-dropping details about the oppression, there just wasn't room to include everything. Trust me, we could write another entire memoir on Doug's experiences.

What can I say about Mark Bolz? Sometimes it took him a while to respond to an inquiry, but each time he did, he reemphasized how supportive he was and how glad he was that this story was being told. Mark is, perhaps, the wittiest person I have ever met, and his humorous analyses and presentations of every situation keep us all in stitches.

By his own admission, Brian Pyle was somewhat isolated from the day-to-day interactions with the EBS elite, so he couldn't provide much input on the questions that I posed to the group. Suffice it to say that he has always been anxious to have this story told, and definitely played a significant role in the actual trial outcome.

Keep in mind that the general scenario related in this story was simultaneously playing itself out in almost every department in the utility. Many of my contributors who were also (reluctantly) members of the "brotherhood" provided their own accounts which, but for the sake of brevity and economy, we could have included in this narrative. Without hesitation, I can say that we took it easy on those who helped implement and execute this very dark period in the history of Chelan County PUD. There is so much more to tell.

The illustrations of Dan McConnell were a tremendous enhancement. The fact that all of the cartoon illustrations we used were produced during the original timeline of the story should be significant to readers. These illustrations reflect the feelings and mindset of the residents of the Wenatchee valley at that time. Each one appeared on the editorial page of the Wenatchee World coincidental with the controversy they related to and I tried to remain true to that timeline when I presented them in the story. Dan is a great artist and I am grateful to have been granted permission to use his illustrations.

Lastly, I believe that I found the right resource to interpret and present this material as a real-life memoir. John DeSimone has been a pleasure to work with and has provided invaluable insight and education on the process of developing a story like this. I sometimes felt apprehensive about inundating him with so much material. Still, he always gleaned the relevant information from each document and article to shape the narrative. I introduced him to online collaborative tools to provide him with material and chapter timelines for review and to send me transcripts and draft chapters for editing. During our phone conversations, some of the most gratifying moments were when he let me ramble while recording the information. There were moments when he would interrupt me and express some incredulity about what he had just heard. It was as if he was picking his jaw up off the floor. Some of the individuals' behavior and attitudes in this story were extremely hard for him to believe. I think those moments will be evident in the book.

After we began this project, some people asked me how long it would take. I told them I had no idea. I knew roughly what I wanted to cover. I told them I had an outline and identified resources, and I had selected a writer. But I couldn't tell them how long it takes to write a book. There are so many variables that I don't think anyone can answer that question. John and I had a target, but the story grew, and we found more material. We revised and re-sequenced things. In the end, it took about twice as long as we anticipated to produce the draft manuscript, and I have no problem with that. I like the way this came out, and I owe that to everyone who contributed.

Thank you from the bottom of my heart.

Ne Oublie – "Never Forget"

Bibliography

Argyris, Chris. *On Organizational Learning*. Malden: Wiley-Blackwell, 1999.

Aristotle. *Nichomachean Ethics*. Translated by Martin Oswald. Upper Saddle River: Prentice Hall, 1999.

Bellman, Geoffrey M. *Getting Things Done When You Are Not In Charge*. New York: Simon & Schuster, 1992.

Boar, Bernard H. *Strategic Thinking for Information Technology*. Hoboken: Wiley, 1996.

Boar Bernard H. *Practical Steps for Aligning Information Technology with Business Strategies: How to Achieve a Competitive Advantage*. Hoboken: Wiley, 1994.

Brymer, George. *Vital Integrities: How Values-Based Leaders Acquire and Preserve Their Credibility*. Toledo: All Square, 2005.

Drucker, Peter F. *The Changing World of the Executive*. New York: Truman Talley Books, 1982.

Freedman, David H. *Corps Business: The 30 Management Principles of the U.S. Marines*. New York: Harper Collins, 2000.

Harrison, Matt. *Leadership Lessons from Sun Tzu and the Art of War*. Read by Nate Sjol. Audible recording. Newark: Audible, 2019.

Ouellette, L. Paul. *I.S. at Your Service: Knowing and Keeping Your Clients*. Dubuque: Kendall Hunt, 1997.

Ouellette, L. Paul. *How to Market the I/S Department*

Internally: Getting the Recognition and Strategic Position You Merit. New York: AMACOM, 1992.

Senge, Peter M. *The Fifth Discipline: The Art & Practice of The Learning Organization.* New York: Currency, 1994.

Senge, Peter M. *The Fifth Discipline Fieldbook: Strategies and Tools for Building a Learning Organization.* New York: Currency, 1994.

Sturdivant, Frederick D. and Heidi Vernon-Wortzel. *Business and Society: A Managerial Approach, 4th Edition.* New York: McGraw-Hill, 1990. q q